To Ty
With l...
Graeme

To Ty
With l...

Graeme

A HAMLYN POINTER BOOK

The SEASHORE

By Jennifer Cochrane

Illustrated by Ken Lilly, Patricia Mynott,
James Nicholls and George Thompson

HAMLYN
LONDON · NEW YORK · SYDNEY · TORONTO

**The illustrations in this book have been selected
from the Hamlyn all-colour paperbacks A GUIDE
TO THE SEASHORE by Ray Ingle, LIFE IN THE SEA
by John Croft, SEASHELLS by Peter Dance and
SEABIRDS by David Saunders**

Published 1973 by
The Hamlyn Publishing Group Limited
London · New York · Sydney · Toronto
Hamlyn House, Feltham, Middlesex, England
© Copyright The Hamlyn Publishing Group Limited 1973
ISBN 0 600 38065 3
Printed by Mateu Cromo, Spain

Contents

Introduction 8

The Changing Seashore 10

The Different Types of Seashore 12

Seashores around the World 14

The Zones of the Beach 18

Floating Food 20

The Rocky Shore 22

Rock Pools 36

Sandy Beaches 39

Muddy Shores 48

Estuaries 50

Groynes, Piers and Rocks 53

Animals that Float near the Shore 54

Animals that Swim near the Shore 56

Mammals on the Seashore 57

Offshore Bottom Dwellers 58

Seabirds 62

Collecting on the Seashore 74

INTRODUCTION

A visit to the seashore is an exciting occasion. For one thing it is usually at holiday times. For another, there is always plenty to do. When you are tired of swimming in the sea, then there are sand-castles to build and rocks to climb on. In the course of these activities it is more than likely that a number of animals, shells and pretty pieces of seaweed will be found. It is interesting to know more about their lives and where they live.

Some of the plants and animals live on the seashore itself. Others may have been left behind by the retreating tide. These animals and plants usually live just offshore, in the part that is always covered with water, but some of them may live in really deep waters and have been washed ashore by a storm.

These deep sea animals are a very exciting find. Nearly three-quarters of the Earth's surface is covered by the sea and even now we know very little about it. The glimpses given to us on the seashore tell us a little more.

The animals and plants that live on the seashore are also very interesting. What makes living creatures choose to live in such a difficult place? It is not as if only a few animals lived there: there are a great many different kinds. Almost every group of *invertebrates* (animals without backbones), has a member living on the seashore. Four of the five main groups of the *vertebrates* (animals with backbones) are also represented. Fishes, reptiles, birds and the furry animals, the mammals, are found on the beaches. There is not such a wide variety of plants. Very few of the flowering plants are found on the seashore. Most of the plants are Algae. Algae are plants without proper leaves, stems and roots. The seaweeds are Algae.

This book describes the kinds of plants and animals likely to be found on the seashore. It is not big

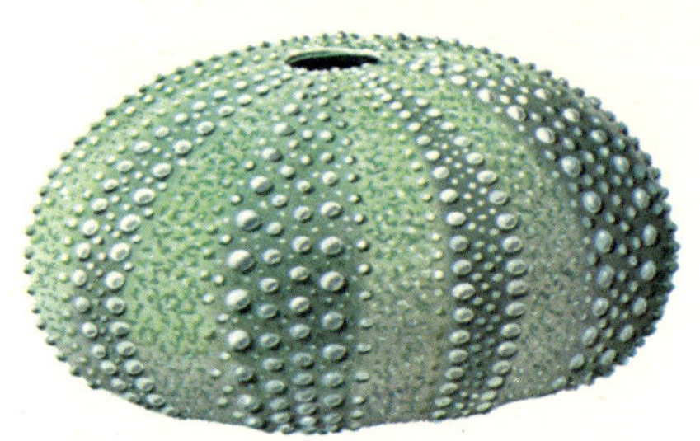

Above: Many bits and pieces are washed up on beaches, and it is usually possible to find the remains of dead animals, such as shells. This is the shell of a sea-urchin *Parechinus angulosus.* It normally lives in the sub-littoral zone. The shells found on the beach have lost all the spines which usually cover them, and the tube-feet which come out through very small holes in the shell.

Right: The Herring Gull *Larus argentatus* is one of the medium sized gulls. It nests in colonies, usually on steep ground at the tops of cliffs. It often lines its nests with seaweed. Herring Gulls feed on fishes, worms, crustaceans, molluscs and almost anything else they can find. They drop molluscs from the air to break their shells. They are found in Europe, Scandinavia and Iceland.

Right: The shells of animals are not easily destroyed when the animal dies. There are large numbers of empty shells to be found on a seashore. On rocky shores there are shells with their owners still inside. This picture shows a few animals that might be found on a rocky beach. The small shells on the rock (*top*) are Acorn Barnacles *Balanus balanoides.* The crab (*top right*) is the Shore crab *Carcinus maenas.* The snail-like shells (*centre*) belongs to the Common Periwinkle *Littorina littorea* and the rayed shells (*bottom*) are Common Limpets *Patella vulgata.*
Plants and animals all have their own scientific names. They have two, like most people, but their 'surname' comes first and has a capital letter, and their own name comes second and begins with a small letter.

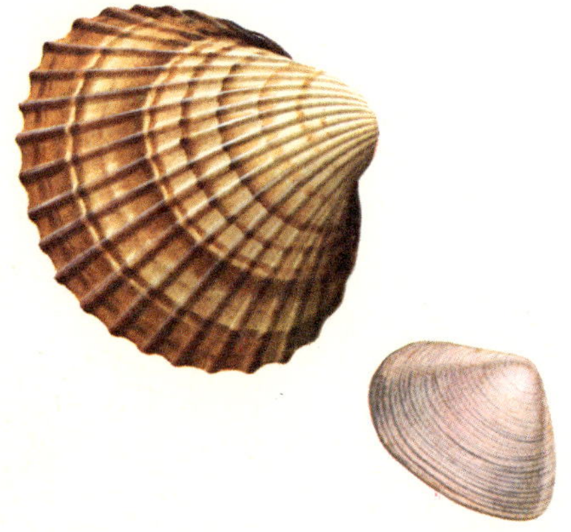

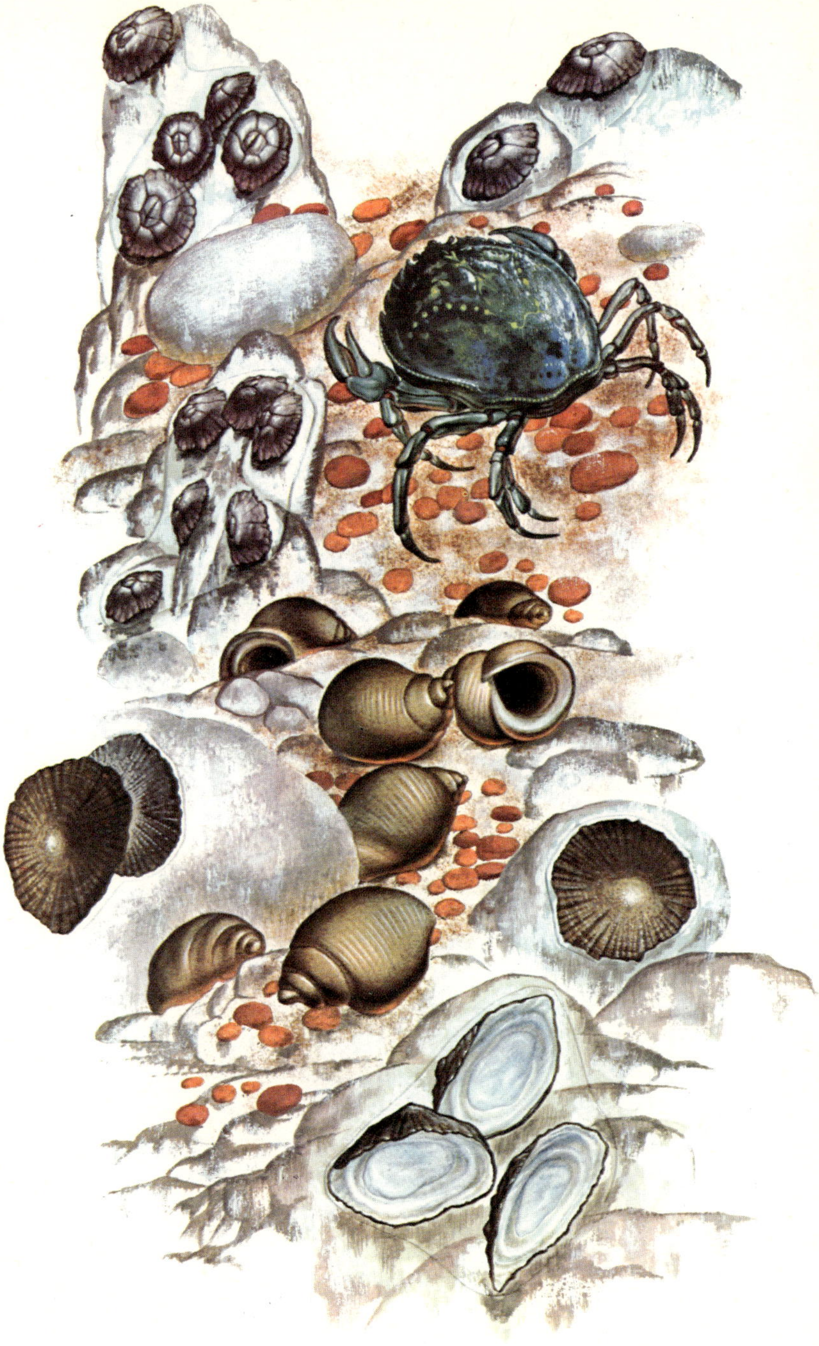

Above: The larger of these two shells is called the Edible Cockle, the European Cockle and the Common Cockle in different places. Scientists call it by its scientific name *Cerastoderma edule* so that everyone knows exactly which cockle they are talking about. The smaller shell is the Baltic Tellin *Macoma balthica.* Both are found on muddy beaches. The cockle lives in sand too.

enough to describe them all, so do not be disappointed if you cannot name everything you find on the beaches from this book. You need books called *keys* to help you to identify plants and animals. You can find keys in libraries if you want to study the subject more deeply. This book will tell you what you are likely to find on the different kinds of beach. You do not find the same things on a sandy beach as you do on a rocky beach. You can tell where an animal or plant has come from by looking at it carefully.

THE CHANGING SEASHORE

The seashores are not the same from one day to another. The incoming tide may bring in more sand or more stones. It may wash some away. Storms fling more shingle up on to the beach and a high wind will blow away some of the loose, dry sand. Some beaches are steadily getting wider and wider, as the incoming tides bring in sand and stones and drop them in the shallow waters by the beach. As the beaches get wider and higher, the tide can no longer cover the top part. Then the wind blows the sand into sand dunes and grass begins to grow on them. As the sand dunes stop moving about, anchored by the grass, so other land plants grow on them and they are no longer part of the beach.

Some beaches are eaten away by the sea. The tides and currents of the sea sweep away the sand and shingle, eating back into the shore until they have changed the shape of the beach. If there are cliffs, the sea will not stop until it has reached them. If the cliffs are made of a soft rock, the sea will eat into the bottom of the cliff, so that it falls into the sea. Even the rocks can be altered. The frosts in the winter freeze the water in the cracks in the rock. The ice expands, the crack widens and in time the piece of rock will fall off. The sea also hurls stones against the rocks during rough weather, chipping off little pieces. So it is that, very slowly, the sea changes the shape of the seashore.

Right: Waves are caused by the wind. The wind pushes the surface of the sea so that the water rises up and rolls over.

Below: The tide and waves move the sand along the beach. The grains of sand roll up the beach and back (*as the arrows show*). The beach is slowly moving to the right in this picture.

Below bottom: Man builds groynes to stop the sand moving too far. The sand is always higher on one side than it is on the other. There is usually a pool on the side that the sand would be moving to. The waves have washed away the sand and the groyne stops sand moving across to fill the space.

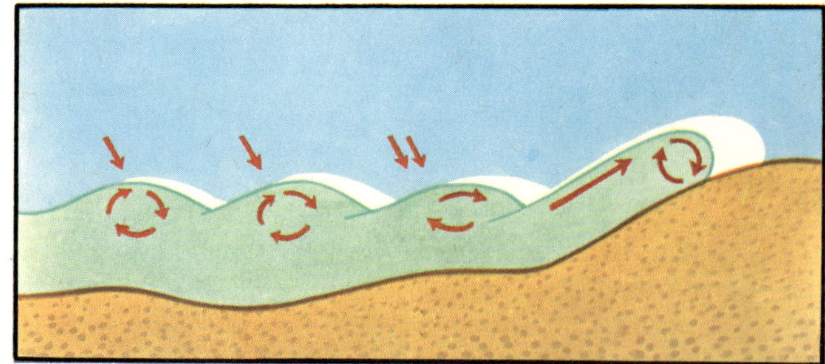

These changes are taking place now, showing us how even today the shape of the land is changing. The seashore is an excellent place to find evidence of the changes that have taken place in the past. How do we find out about the lands of millions of years ago? We study the rocks to find out whether they were made on land or under the sea. We look for fossils, which tell us what kinds of animals were alive then. It is quite difficult to find naked rocks inland. They are usually covered by a layer of earth. Unless they are uncovered by engineers making a road, or some other, similar, circumstance the only places to see bare rocks are up mountains or by the sea. So the seashore is as much a hunting ground for the animals of the past as

Right: These cliffs were once at the bottom of an ocean. They are made from the skeletons of tiny one-celled animals, which were alive millions of years ago, living in the plankton.

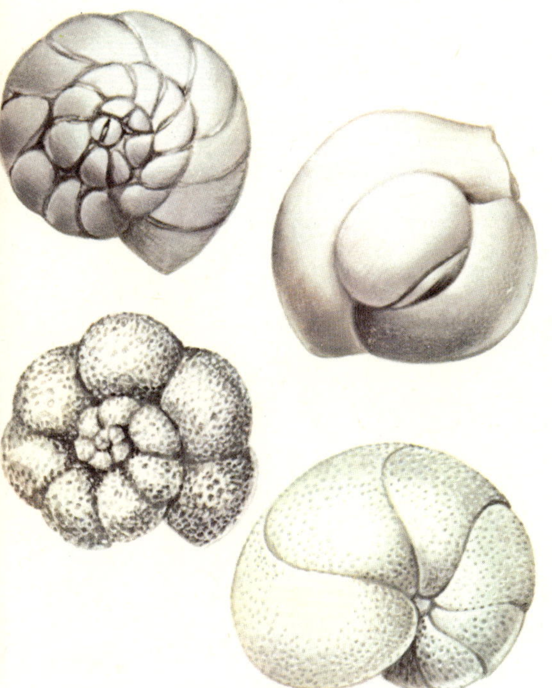

Above: These are the shells of the animals that make up the cliffs (in the above picture). There are animals like them still living today. They are called foraminiferans. You need a powerful magnifying glass to see them. If you look at sand from a beach near cliffs like this through the glass, you may be able to find some.

it is for the present-day inhabitants. The evidence for the way the seashore has changed can be found in the rocks.

Some of these past seashore dwellers are easier to see than others. The great limestone cliffs not only contain fossils, they are made up completely from fossils. These cliffs are evidence that this part of the land was once the sea bed of some great, quiet ocean. It was once covered by water and well away from the shore. The cliffs are made from the fossilized skeletons of millions of tiny floating animals. These little one-celled animals are called foraminifera. They have skeletons rather like very small seashells made of calcium. They lived then, and still do live, in the sea. It must have been very still where they lived, because the shells were not tossed about by the waves and broken up. When the animals died, the shells rained quietly down to the bottom of the sea. This happened for a very long time, because a thick layer of white mud was made by the skeletons. After millions of years the deposit grew so thick that the weight of the top layers compressed the bottom layers and formed rock. Then a great upheaval took place on the Earth's surface, and the seabed was pushed up to make dry land. The dry land eventually bordered the sea again, and the sea ate away the rock to make the great white cliffs that can be seen today.

THE DIFFERENT TYPES OF SEASHORE

The edges of the land are not all the same. The rocks which come down to the sea may be hard or soft. They may be covered by earth. They may slope gently to the water's edge, or tower above it. If the rocks slope down to the water, then the sea can cover them with a thick layer of sand and shingle. If they are soft, the sea will wear them away, and grind them up to make shingle and sand. In some parts of the world the rocky cliffs plunge down into the sea without a ledge that can be called a beach. In other places, the rocks shelter coves of smooth sand which are completely covered when the tide comes in. Rivers run into the sea where the land is flat. They bring mud downstream from

Below: There is no beach at all in some places. The picture shows how the rocky cliffs plunge down into the sea. There will be some seaweeds growing at the base of the cliffs and some molluscs and barnacles will probably live there, but there will be fewer living things than there would be on a shallow beach.

Below: This picture shows five different kinds of seashore. There are rocky parts with cliffs, sandy parts, shingly parts, muddy parts and the estuary. The plants and animals which live on these different beaches will be discussed in this book.

the fields, and the seashores in estuaries are often muddy. There are, in fact, a large variety of seashores, but they can be divided into three main types. They may be rocky or sandy or they may be muddy.

On each of these different kinds of shore different groups of animals and plants are found. A group of animals and plants that live together is called a community. Each kind of seashore has a typical community.

The rocky shore is the most interesting shore at first glance, for two reasons. The first is that animals cannot hide by burying themselves on a rocky shore. Very few animals can bore into rock. The second is that seaweeds need a firm surface to which to attach themselves. Seaweeds do not have roots like flowering plants; they fasten themselves to stones or rocks with a *holdfast*. The holdfast cannot fasten itself into sand and so seaweeds do not grow on sand. Rocky shores, however, unless they are frequently lashed by violent waves, have a thick cover of sea-weeds.

Above: This warm, shallow sandy beach looks empty but there are plenty of animals buried in the sand and living in the sea. This kind of beach is best seen with a mask and flippers. The most interesting part is under the shallow water.

Above: Not all seashores are warm and sandy. It is not possible to see the land at all on this seashore. It is covered with ice. There are still a great many animals and plants to be found, however. The sea has many tiny creatures floating in it, and there are fishes swimming in the sea.

Sandy and muddy shores look empty at first glance. In fact there are a great many animals living on a sandy shore, but they are all buried deep in the sand, protected from the heat of the sun and the drying air when the tide is out, and from the beating waves as the tide comes in. When the tide is in and there is water over the sand, then the animals rise to the surface to feed, but they disappear very quickly at the sound of footsteps.

A muddy shore has the same characteristics as a sandy shore; it looks dead at first. It has plenty of life on it, but it is all under the surface. There may be plants on a muddy shore, however, as the only marine flowering plant, eel-grass, grows there.

SEASHORES AROUND THE WORLD

The seashores are typical of the part of the world in which they are situated. A seashore on a Pacific island is quite different from a seashore in a Norwegian fiord. The icy Antarctic seas hold plants and animals which are quite unlike those in the Indian Ocean. One of the factors that affect the seashore is the temperature in the part of the world in which it is situated. The other important factor is the current that sweeps the shores.

The temperature is the most obvious influence. It will be colder at the North and South Poles than it is in the temperate parts of the world, and it will be much hotter at the Equator than it is anywhere else. The water in the polar seas will be cooled down by the ice and the water in the equatorial waters will be warmed by the sun.

The movements of the water round the world are very complicated. The spin of the Earth and the prevailing winds send great currents of water swirling through the seas and oceans. These currents take

Below: This map shows the different regions of the world. Each coloured region has its own group of plants and animals living in it. The living things in one region do not all live in the region next to it, perhaps because it is too cold for them to survive, or there is not enough of their kind of food. Some regions are too far apart to have the same plants or animals living in them. Some seeds or eggs are carried across oceans by currents, so that they are found on both sides of the body of water.

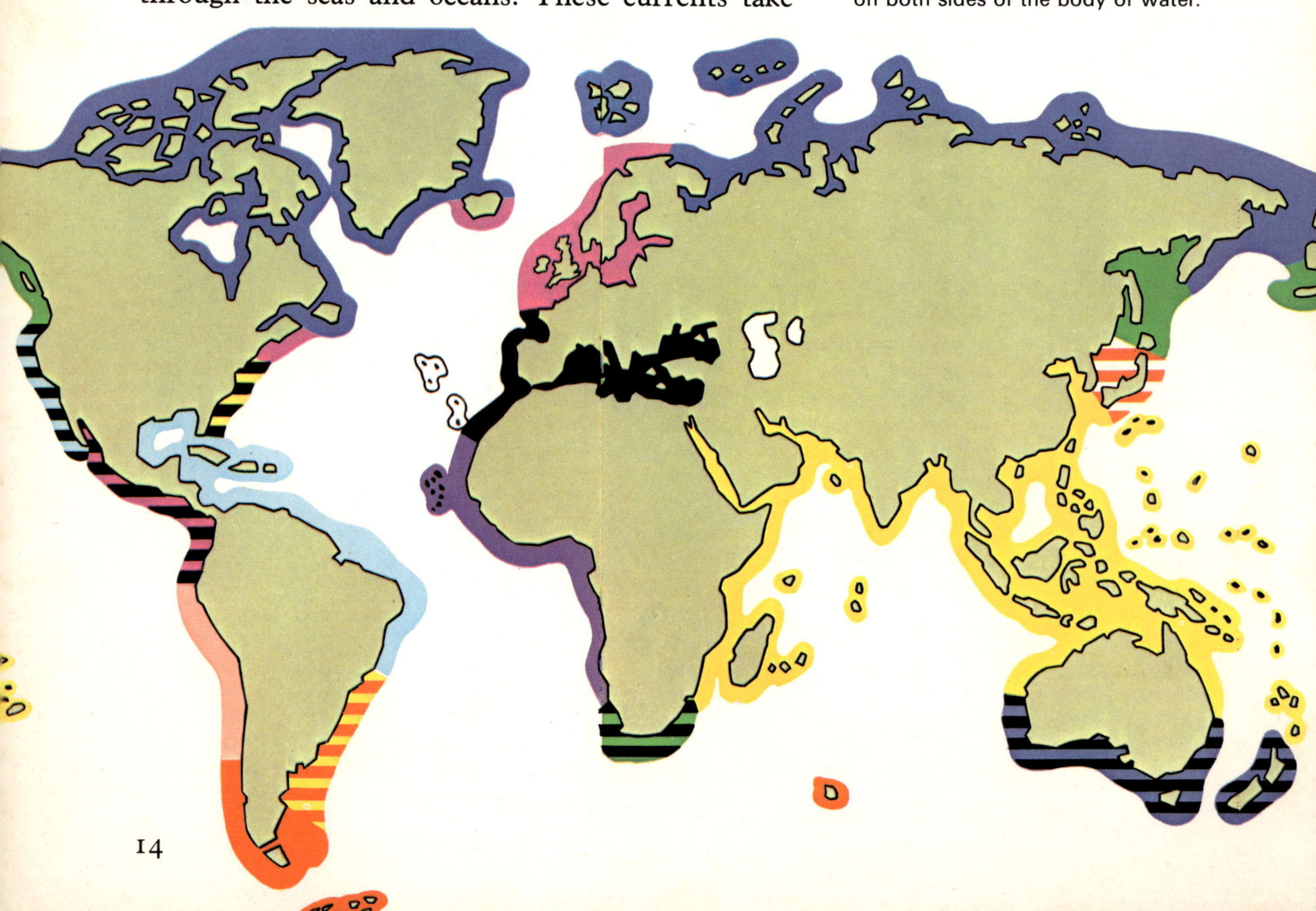

Right: The Queen Conch *Strombus gigas* lives in the Caribbean region (*coloured pale blue on the map on the page opposite*). It is found in the shallow waters near the shore, where there are coral reefs. The Queen Conch is a typical warm water creature with its spiky shell and its bright colours.

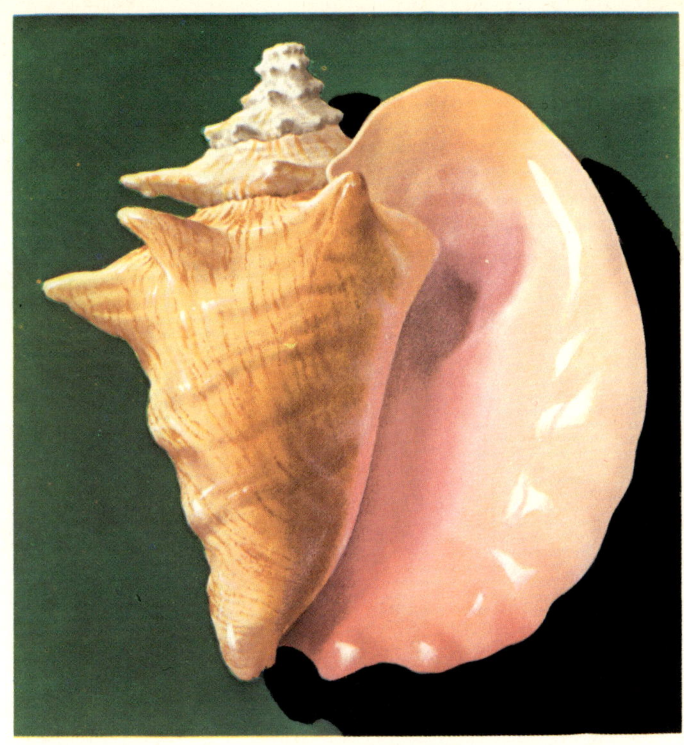

warm waters into cool areas and cold waters into warmer regions. They also carry plants and animals about in them, distributing them about the world. These currents of water affect the climate of the lands they border. The climate of Great Britain is changed by the North Atlantic Drift, a current of water moving from the Caribbean sea across the North Atlantic to Northern Europe. This current is also called the Gulf Stream. It warms the seas round Great Britain, making it a warmer, wetter place than it would be without it. It also carries seeds and shells across the ocean and deposits them on the shores of Britain and Ireland.

These differences in temperature and position of the various seashores mean that there are regions which have their own communities in them. These are called biogeographical regions by the biologists.

Below: This tellin *Strigilla carnaria* is another of the molluscs found in the Caribbean region. It is found on sandy shores, buried in the sand. Like the Queen Conch, the tellin is brightly coloured, which is typical of animals living in warm waters.

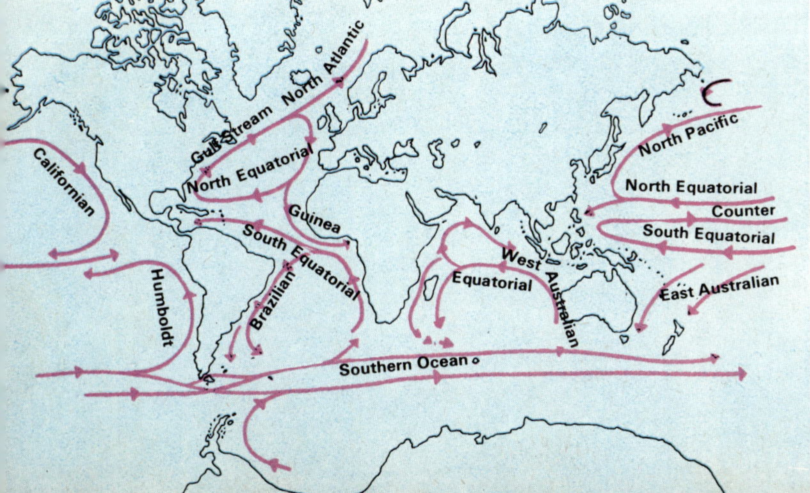

Left: This map shows the paths of the currents of water that sweep round the oceans on the surface of the water. If the map is compared with the one on the opposite page, it can be seen that there is some connection between the currents and the regions. The currents carry seeds and animals in them. If these arrive on a suitable shore at the correct temperature, they may well grow there.

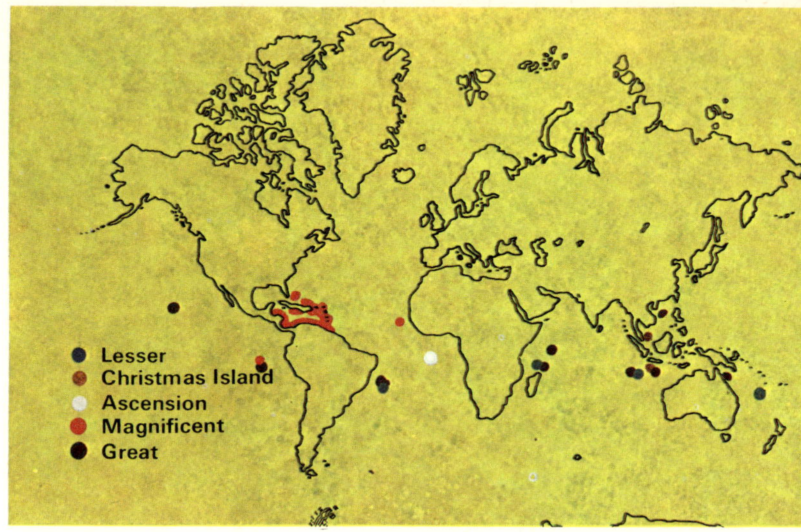

Each region has its own particular collection of plants and animals, and if the animal is one that cannot move far by itself, then it is not likely to be found anywhere but in its own region. Animals such as birds, which can fly for long distances, are not always found in only one region. The factors that decide which plants and animals will be able to live in which region are things like the warmth and the number of hours of daylight, as well as the salts available in the water to help the plants make their food.

It is not always warm in the places one would expect it to be warm. The movements of the currents in the sea are very complicated. Cold water is heavier than warm water, so that it is usually on the bottom. Fresh water is lighter than salt water, however, even when it is cold. Because of this it is possible to have a current of warm, salty water, moving in one direction, sandwiched between a current of cold salty water at the bottom and cold fresh water at the top, each moving in a different direction from the warm water. It is this curious set of circumstances that makes the Antarctic a place in which a great many plants and animals can live. The cold fresh water comes from the ice.

The water off the west coast of South America is not as warm as one might expect it to be. This is because the cold current called the West Wind Drift that sweeps round Antarctica is divided by the land mass of South America, and part of the current of water flows up the western coast of the country. This current is the famous Humboldt Current, on which Thor Heyerdahl began his voyage on the Kon Tiki.

It is possible, to some extent, to tell by looking at an animal whether it is a warm water or a cold water creature. On the whole, animals that live in cold waters are not as brightly coloured as those found in

warm waters. They tend to be silvery grey, brown and white. They are usually larger than similar warm water animals, with smaller feet. There are a few exceptions, of course, but as a general rule it is true.

The warm water animals are gaily coloured and have many more spines and decorations on them than those in cool waters. The animals living in the warm parts of the world are often very beautiful. This is particularly true of the molluscs. The seashells from the Indian Ocean and the Asian coasts are very colourful and have intricately graceful shapes. Whatever the form of the animal, however, it is likely to live very much like its counterpart in colder regions living in the same type of shore.

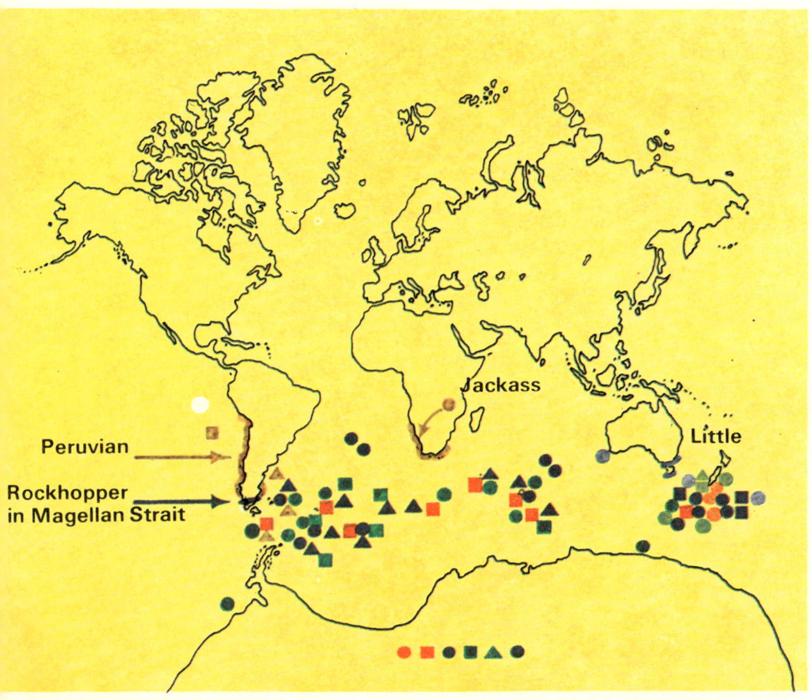

THE ZONES OF THE BEACH

The beach is divided into zones. The zones are recognized both by their position on the beach and by the communities of plants and animals living in them. There are five possible zones, but some of these may be run together if the beach has a very gentle slope.

One of the things that divides the beach is the tides. Twice a day the tides come in all over the world. Twice a day they go out again, leaving the beach exposed to the sun and wind. The top of the beach is only covered with salt water for a short time. The plants and animals living there have to be able to live through long, dry periods. The bottom of the beach is only uncovered for a short time. The community spends only a short time out of water. All the living things on the beach have to be able to withstand the waves crashing down on them, or to find a sheltered part of the beach.

The animals and plants which are exposed to the air for a long time have another problem to contend with. They get rained on. This is no problem for land animals, but it is a considerable one for aquatic ones. Marine creatures cannot live in fresh water and freshwater animals cannot live in salt water. Anything living in a pool on a beach in a rainstorm is likely to find itself in fresh water. So, apart from the difficulties of sun and wind, the seashore communities have to survive rain. The extent to which the living things are able to survive in these different conditions governs their position on the beach, and the zone they are likely to be found in.

The five zones on the seashore are the splash zone, the upper shore zone, the middle shore zone, the lower shore zone and the sub-littoral zone. The

Above: The brown seaweeds called wracks show zoning very well. Bladder Wrack *Fucus vesiculosus* (*right*) grows in the middle shore zone of a rocky beach. The seaweed on the left is Serrated Wrack *Fucus serratus* which grows on the lower shore zone. The zones higher up the beach also have their typical wracks.

Right: This diagram shows the five zones of the seashore. It is shown here on a sandy beach, but the zones show up best on a rocky beach, where seaweeds grow thickly. The zones are related to the tides. The upper shore is covered by water only at the spring high tides. The lower shore is only uncovered at spring low tides.

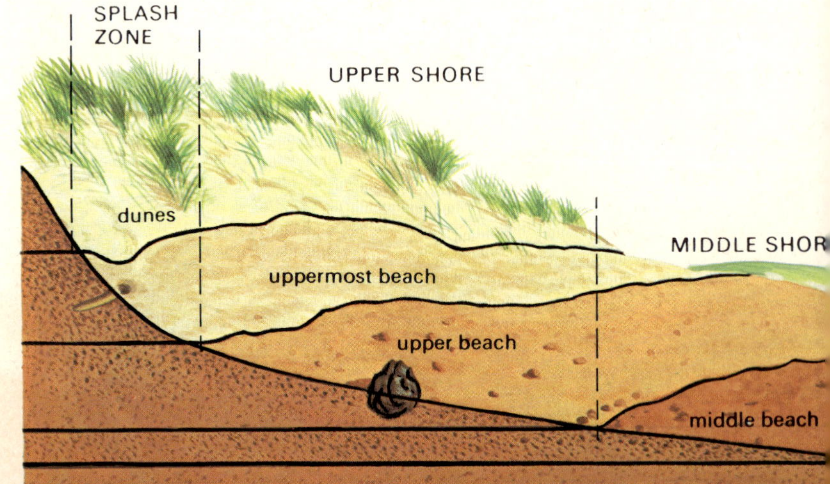

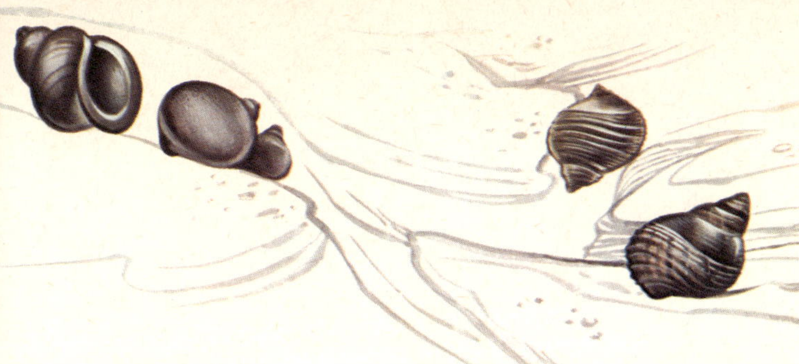

splash zone is never covered by water, the sub-littoral zone is never uncovered. The upper shore zone is only covered at high tide, the lower shore zone is only uncovered at low tide and the middle shore zone spends about half the time under water.

Many of the splash zone community are land animals, but are able to live in the very salty conditions of this zone. There are a fairly large number of flowering plants found in the higher parts of the splash zone.

The upper shore zone has a fairly large community living in it, but the dry conditions limit the size to some extent. It is in the middle and lower shore zones that the abundance of living things usually associated with the seashore appears. Here, the combination of enough mineral salts for the plants to make food, with plenty of sunlight and sufficient oxygen, seems to outweigh the disadvantages and produces a great variety of plants and animals.

The sub-littoral zone is underwater all the time, but the water covering it may be shallow. There are plenty of fishes as well as all the groups found further up the beach and it is a rewarding place in which to hunt for seashore life.

These zones show up best on rocky beaches. It is with the rocky beach communities that we will begin.

Above: The periwinkles are animals which show zoning very clearly. They are found on rocky beaches. The diagram shows their positions on the beach. The Small Periwinkle *Littorina neritoides* lives in the splash zone and the upper shore zone. The Rough Periwinkle, *Littorina saxalis* lives in the upper and middle shore zones. The Flat Periwinkle *Littorina littoralis* and the Edible Periwinkle *Littorina littorea* are both found in the middle and lower shore zones.

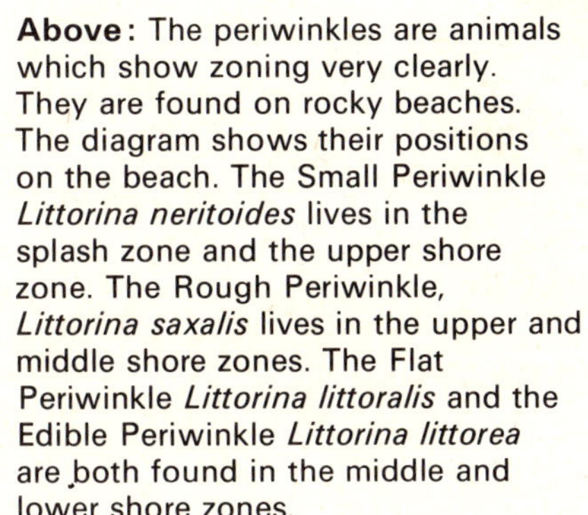

Above: Oarweed *Laminaria digitata* grows in the lower shore zone and in the sub-littoral zone. It is rarely exposed to the air, and it grows in fairly deep water.

FLOATING FOOD

All living things need energy to live. They need energy to make any movements at all, even breathing movements, and they need energy to grow and reproduce. All the energy used on Earth comes from the Sun. Plants are able to convert the energy of the Sun into food. They do this with *chlorophyll*, the green colour in plants. Animals can only acquire energy by eating plants or by eating other animals. They cannot make food themselves as the plants can. It is possible to draw a pyramid, with the energy-producers, the plants, at the bottom and all the animals that depend on the plants above them. The top of the pyramid is usually a large animal, such as a dolphin, which is not eaten by anything else.

In order to make food plants need sunlight, carbon dioxide, water and mineral salts. Mineral salts are not just the salt used by Man on his food. There are many others. The sea is full of them. They are what makes the sea salty. The plants in the sea, therefore, have plenty of water and carbon dioxide, plenty of salts and quite a lot of sunlight. It is not surprising that there are a great many plants on the sea's surface. Some of these plants are the great seaweeds. They are easy to see, but many, many more of them are so small that they can only be seen with a microscope. They float in the top layers of the seas and they are found all over the world. They are the source of all the energy in the oceans. These tiny floating plants are

Below: These are some of the minute plants that float in the sea near the shore. They are called phytoplankton. Two of them are diatoms named (*a*) *Chaetoceros decipiens* and (*b*) *Biddulphia regia*. The other three are dinoflagellates. Their names are (*c*) *Noctiluca scintillans*, (*d*) *Ceratium tridos* and (*e*) *Perindium depressum*. *Noctiluca* is a phosphorescent plant. That means that it shines in the dark. Sometimes the wake behind a ship glows in the dark. It is often *Noctiluca* which causes this.

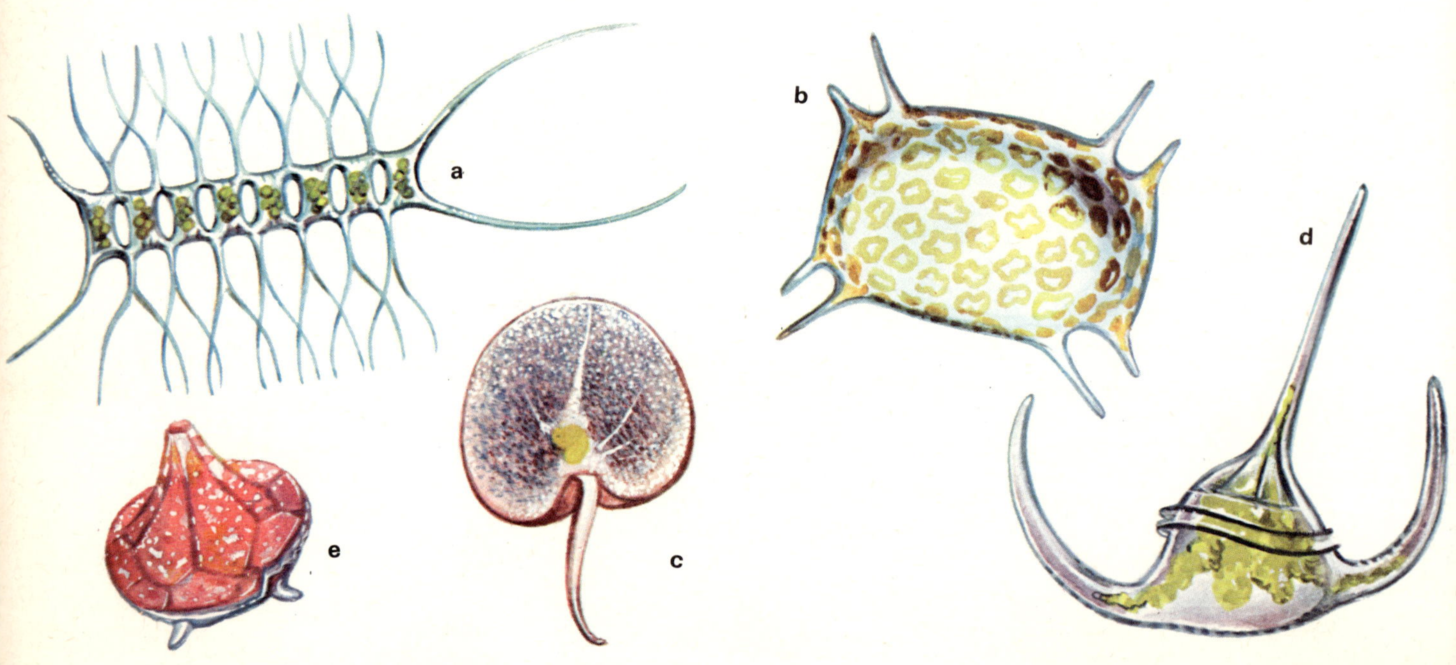

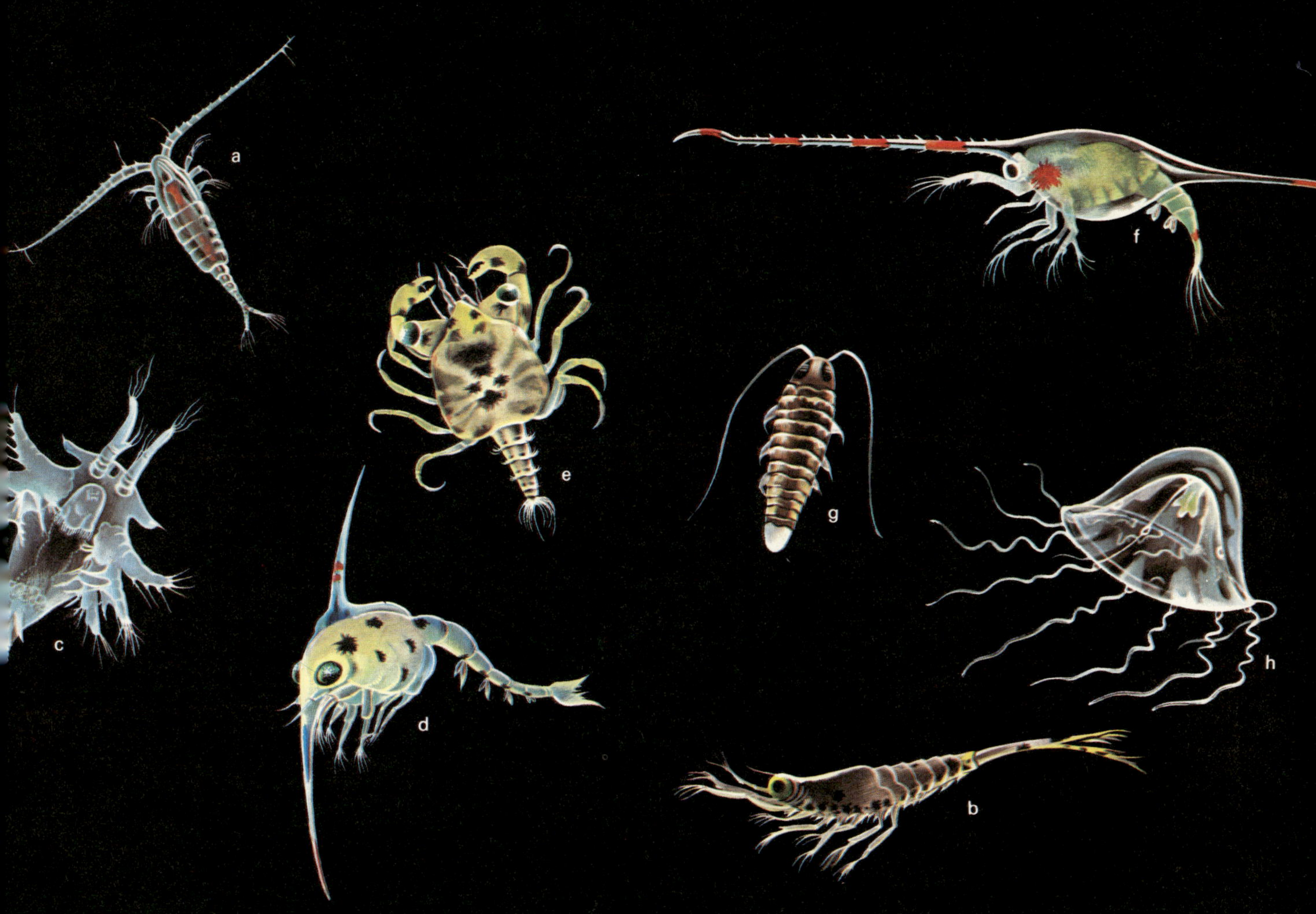

called phytoplankton. They are the 'grass of the sea'.

The phytoplankton are all Algae. They are one-celled plants and they are often very beautiful. They may be green or yellow or red. Some of them have small skeletons surrounding them, fitting round them like date boxes or cheese boxes. They may have spines or strange shell-like shapes.

The water off the shore is thick with phytoplankton. The animals living in it are living in a soup which they can eat. They do not have to wander about looking for their food. Many of them are actually sitting in it for most of the time. The floating food is not all phytoplankton. There are one-celled animals floating about too, feeding on the plants. These one-celled animals are called protozoans. They are also very beautiful if they are seen under a microscope. They may have skeletons made of lime or the stuff that sand is made from, shaped like tiny seashells or like spiky balls.

There are other animals living in the soupy sea-water. There are the young of many of the animals which live on the shore. Molluscs, crustaceans and many other groups have larvae swimming about in the water offshore, forming part of the floating food.

Above: There are a great many animals floating about in the floating food in the sea. Some of them are protozoans, but many are the larvae of shore animals or animals that usually spend their lives in one place. Most of the animals shown in this picture are crustaceans: (*a*) *Calanus finmarchicus*, is a copepod. These are the smallest crustaceans; (*b*) the larva of the Brown Shrimp *Crangon vulgaris*; (*c*) the larva of the crustacean that looks like a mollusc, *Balanus balanoides*, the barnacle; (*d*) and (*e*) different stages in the life of the Shore Crab, *Carcinus maenas*; (*f*) one of the stages in the life of the Porcelain Crab, *Porcellana longicornis*; (*g*) an isopod, one of the crustaceans related to the woodlice, named *Eurydice pulchra*; (*h*) not a crustacean, but a larva of one of the sea-anemone family *Clytia johnstoni*.

THE ROCKY SHORE

THE SPLASH ZONE AND UPPER SHORE

The plants in the splash zone of a rocky shore are mostly lichens. Lichens are strange plants which are a mixture of Fungi and Algae. The Fungus part of the plant is able to fasten itself to the bare rock, while the Alga makes the food. At the top of the splash zone there are some salt-tolerant land plants, which have rooted in the soil caught in crevices in the rock. Some are the kind of plants which are able to conserve their water. They are called xerophytes. Sea-campion, Sea-lavender, Thrift and Scots-lovage are a few of the plants likely to grow in the splash zone.

Many of the animals found in this zone are land animals that have wandered down to the seashore. Various insects, such as beetles and flies, may be found here, which are not permanent members of the splash zone community. The seashore animals which live in this zone are the Sea Slater and the Small Periwinkle.

The upper shore zone is covered by the sea at high tide. The true seaweeds first appear in this zone. The green seaweeds, which are able to withstand the strong light and the long dry periods, are usually more common than the other two groups of seaweeds,

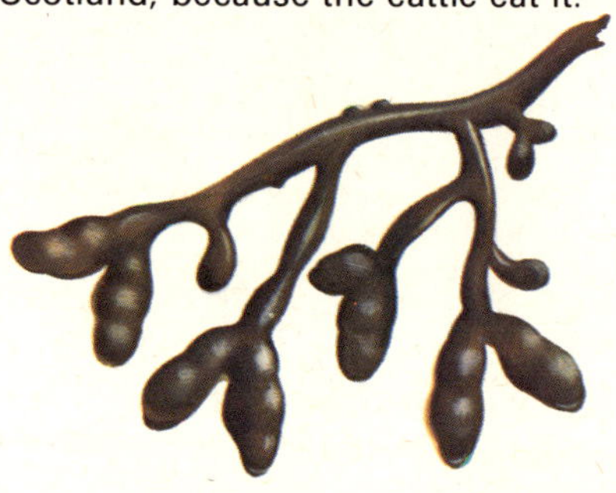

Below: Channelled Wrack, *Pelvetia canaliculata*, grows on the upper shore zone of a rocky beach. It becomes black when it is exposed to the air for long periods. It is found on sheltered parts of the beach. This seaweed is called Cow Tang in Scotland, because the cattle eat it.

Below: Spiral Wrack, *Fucus spiralis* grows below Channelled Wrack. Like this wrack, Spiral Wrack is found on sheltered shores. There are many more animals to be found hiding in Spiral Wrack than there are in Channelled Wrack.

Left: (*Left*) Intestine weed, *Enteromorpha intestinalis.* Its fronds may grow as long as 60cm. They are sometimes blown up to look like a long balloon. (*Right*) Sea Lettuce *Ulva lactuca.* This seaweed may be found in pools on the beach. It is also common on sandy and muddy beaches. Both these seaweeds can tolerate fresh water.

the red seaweeds and the brown seaweeds. The green
seaweeds are able to withstand the fresh water that
trickles down the beach from streams and also comes
down in rainstorms. Intestine-weed, a bright green,
tube-like weed, is often found actually growing in the
path of streams on the beach. There are some brown
seaweeds in this zone, but no red seaweeds can live so
far up the beach. Channelled Wrack grows at the top
of the upper shore zone and Flat Wrack is found in
large quantities further down towards the middle
shore zone. If the beach is exposed to crashing waves,
then not many seaweeds are found, because the waves
tear them from the rocks. If the rocks are in a sheltered
bay, then the weeds will probably be very thick.

The most obvious animals in the upper shore zone
are the Acorn Barnacles. They are found on bare
rocks; they do not need to shelter underneath seaweeds. The limpets are also found on bare rocks. They
can easily withstand the beating of the waves, with
their thick shells and strong muscles. The rest of the
animals on this part of the shore are found under the
seaweeds. Periwinkles, sandhoppers and millions of
other small creatures may be found in the holdfasts
of the seaweeds.

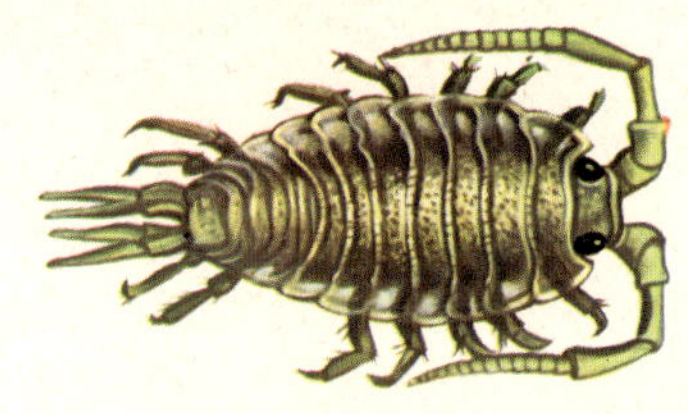

Above: The Sea Slater is found in
the splash zone as well as further
down the beach. This little animal is
rarely seen in the daylight. It comes
out at night to scavenge on the shore
at low tide.

Above: These are two of the many
species of barnacle: (*left*) the Acorn
Barnacle *Balanus balanoides*;
(*right*) *Chthamalus stellatus*. When
these two animals live on the same
beach, *Chthamalus* is found higher
up than *Balanus*, sometimes almost
up into the splash zone.

Right: This is a typical rocky shore,
with rocky outcrops sheltering sandy
coves. The rocks have a seaweed
cover in which many live animals
can be found. There are living
molluscs found crawling on the rocks.

THE MIDDLE SHORE ZONE

The middle shore is covered by the sea for about half the time. The middle shore community does not need to be as resistant to drying as the community that lives further up the shore. There are many more plants and animals in this zone than there are in the upper shore.

Green and brown seaweeds are found growing on the rocks on the middle shore and red seaweeds are found in the rock pools. There are three wracks found here, Spiral Wrack at the top of the zone, Knotted Wrack in the middle and Bladder Wrack at the bottom. Bladder Wrack is the seaweed with little balloons in its fronds; its other name is pop-weed because it is fun to pop the bladders. The red seaweeds cannot stand long periods out of water, so they are only found in rock pools. Most of the seaweeds have feathery red fronds, but one of the most interesting has flat, forked fronds with straight ends. It is called Caragheen, and it turns green in bright sunlight. It is used in the preparation of food. Some ice-cream has Caragheen in it.

There are a great many limpets found in the middle shore zone, and several periwinkles, including the Edible Winkle. The pretty, conical shells of the top-shells can be seen here too. These animals crawl

Above: The Knotted Wrack *Ascophyllum nodosum* is a middle shore wrack. If the plant is studied carefully, it may be possible to see sea-mat growing on it. It looks like a brown crust covering the seaweed. Under a strong hand lens, it is possible to see the separate animals living in their little boxes. This species is *Flustrella hispida*.

Below: Some of the brown seaweeds that might be found on the middle shore, growing on rocks or in pools. The seaweeds do not have common names and have to be referred to by their scientific ones. These are: (*a*) *Chordaria flagelliformis*, (*b*) *Leathesia difformis*, (*c*) *Asperococcus fistulosis*, (*d*) *Ectocarpus confervoides*, (*e*) *Scytosiphon lomentaria* and (*f*) *Chorda filum*.

Below: Bladder Wrack *Fucus vesiculosus* is found on the middle shore. It is easily recognized by the small bladders in its fronds. It grows to a length of 120cm and is a strong seaweed, often found on exposed coasts.

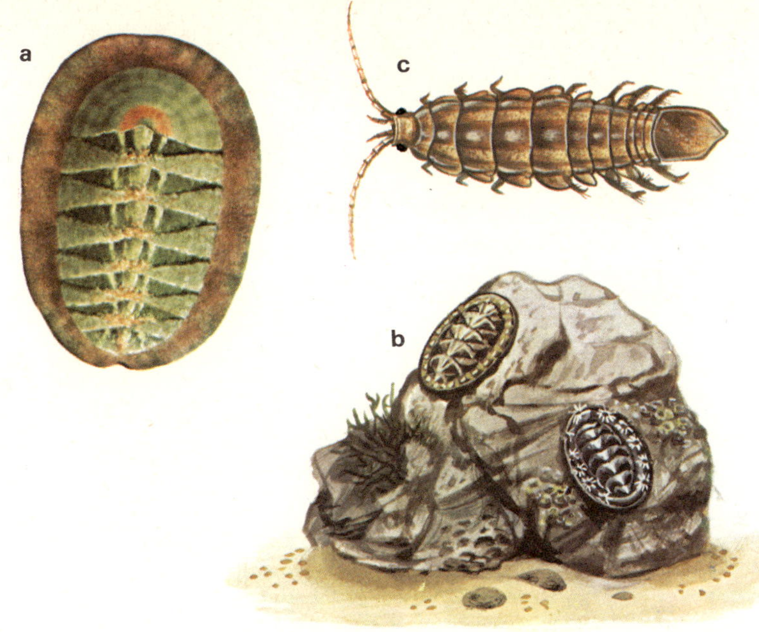

Left: The chitons are very strange-looking molluscs: (*a*) an Australian chiton *Loricella angasi.* It clamps itself to the rocks like the British species (shown in (*b*)); (*c*) the crustacean *Idotea granulosa* which is found hiding among the seaweeds.

Below: The Common Limpet, *Patella vulgata,* is found on most rocky shores. It can survive on very exposed shores as its thick shell can withstand the waves. Many seabirds feed on limpets.

across the rocks, rasping off the Algae with their rough tongues. Not all the molluscs are plant-eaters, however. The Dog Whelk is found in this zone, feeding on the limpets, topshells and periwinkles. The other type of mollusc found in this zone is the chiton. Another name for this animal is the Coat-of-Mail. They are found in crevices or on the underside of rocks, clamped to the surface like a limpet. They have a line of plates down the middle of their backs instead of one shell. If they are knocked off the rocks, they roll up like a woodlouse.

Most of the animals in this zone will be found under the seaweeds or on the underside of rocks, in the shade or in a rock pool. In the more protected places it may be possible to find sponges, corals and sea-squirts. There will also be worms in the holdfasts.

Left: There are a large number of red seaweeds growing on the rock and in the pools in the middle shore zone, and on the fronds of brown seaweeds. The three shown here can be found in rock pools and on rocks. (*Left*) *Porphyra umbilicalis* looks a little like red Sea Lettuce. It may be found on exposed shores. (*Centre*) *Gelidium corneum,* and *Cystoclonium purpureum* (*right*) both have the feathery fronds often found in red seaweeds.

THE LOWER SHORE ZONE

The lower shore zone of a rocky beach is one of the most exciting parts of the seashore. The seaweeds have a firm base upon which to grow and provide plenty of thick fronds for the animals to hide in. There are plenty of animals to look at and they cannot dig themselves into the rock as soon as they feel a tremor caused by a footstep. A patient searcher can look in crevices, under the overhang of rocks and amid the seaweed, and find a great many animals. One of the reasons for the great number of animals is that the lower shore zone is only fully exposed to the sun and wind during the spring tide low water.

The tides move up the beach and retreat down the beach twice a day. They do not, however, always go up and recede again to the same place. This is because the height of the tides is affected by the position of the Moon. Twice a month, the Sun, the Moon and the Earth are in a straight line. This is at new moon, when the Moon is between the Sun and the Earth and at full moon, when the Earth is between the Moon and the Sun. During these times there is a much greater pull on the oceans and seas of the Earth. Just after this the tides come in to a higher level and go out to a lower level. More beach is exposed at low tide than at other times in the month. These large tides are called spring tides. In between these large tides there are two small tides. These tides come just after the first and third quarters of the Moon. They are called neap tides.

The lower shore zone is uncovered at the spring tides and for a short time before and after them. It can only be seen for a short time in each month, but it is well worth waiting for.

Opposite page: Serrated Wrack, or
Toothed Wrack as it is sometimes
called, is the lower shore Wrack. Its
scientific name is *Fucus serratus.*
Its fronds reach 150cm in length.
It grows on exposed shores, but well
down into the water, so that it is not
battered by the waves too much.

Green, brown and red seaweeds all grow in the
lower shore zone. The zone has its own wrack, like
the other zones. Serrated Wrack is found at the top of
the lower shore zone, and at the bottom of the middle
shore zone. There are several other brown seaweeds,
of which thong weed is one of those most easily
recognized. Thong weed has long straps growing out
of a button. Pod weed is another you can easily
recognize. It has long pods on the ends of its fronds.
When the tide is right out, the very large brown seaweeds, the oarweeds, can just be seen. There are a
few green seaweeds in this region, and so many red
seaweeds that it is not possible to describe them all.
Both the green and the red seaweeds sound very much
alike if they are described, in any case. Many of them
are very small and have feathery fronds. The best
way to get to know them is to go down to the beach
with a key, and name them for yourself.

There are a great many different kinds of animals to
be found in this zone. First, there are the sea-snails,
whose scientific name is the gastropod molluscs.
The plant-eating gastropod molluscs, such as the
Common Limpet, the White Tortoiseshell Limpet,
the periwinkles and the topshells are abundant in

Left: Both these red seaweeds may
be found growing on other seaweeds.
They grow to about 15 or 20cm.
Phycodrys rubens (*left*), is sometimes called Sea Oak because of its
Oaktree-leaf-like fronds. *Nitophyllum
punctatum* (*right*) must be handled
with care as its fronds tear easily.

Left: There are many gastropod molluscs to be found on the seashore. The Dog Whelks (*a*) *Nucella lapillus* are meat-eaters, feeding on plant-eaters like the Painted Topshell (*b*), *Zizyphinus zizyphinus.* The star-fishes feed on molluscs. The Cushion Star (*c*), *Asterina gibbosa,* is found on the sides of rocks and boulders. It is a filter feeder as well as a mollusc-eater, like the sea-squirts, (*d*) *Botryllus schlosseri,* which sieve food from the water.

Below: The holdfasts of the sea-weeds are the homes of the worms. The Boot-lace Worm (*a*), *Lineus longissimus* may grow to 450cm long. *Lineus ruber* (*b*) only grows to about 22cm. *Amphiporus lactifloreus* (*c*) is much smaller, only about 7cm. None of these worms has a ringed body, like the ragworm. This is one way of recognising them. They are all meat-eaters and will feed on other worms.

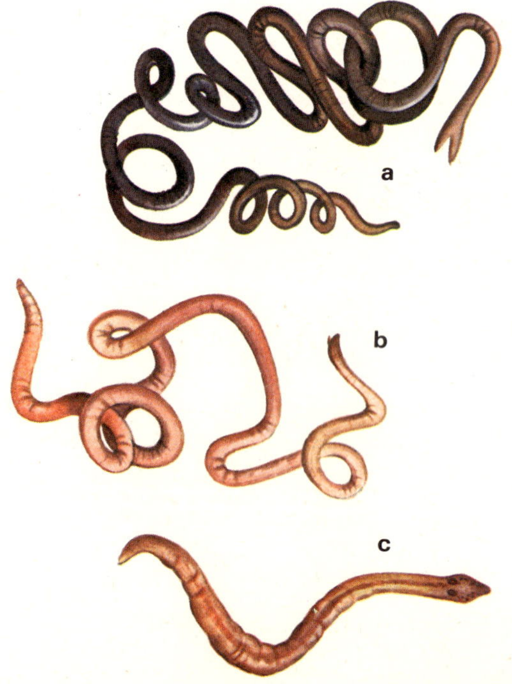

this region. The meat-eating gastropod molluscs, such as the Common Whelk and the Dog Whelk are also present.

The rocks often have small blobs of jelly in crevices and on overhangs. These are usually coloured dark red. They are the anemones with their tentacles pulled inside their bodies, waiting for the return of the waters.

The seaweeds themselves have animals hiding in or on them. The holdfasts of the seaweeds are made from a number of tough root-like branches, clinging to the surface of the rock. There is often room round these branches for worms to shelter, and other small creatures. There are some very long, thin worms. They are called nemertines, or ribbon worms. Then there are some smaller, smoother whitish coloured worms, called nematodes. Nematodes are found in

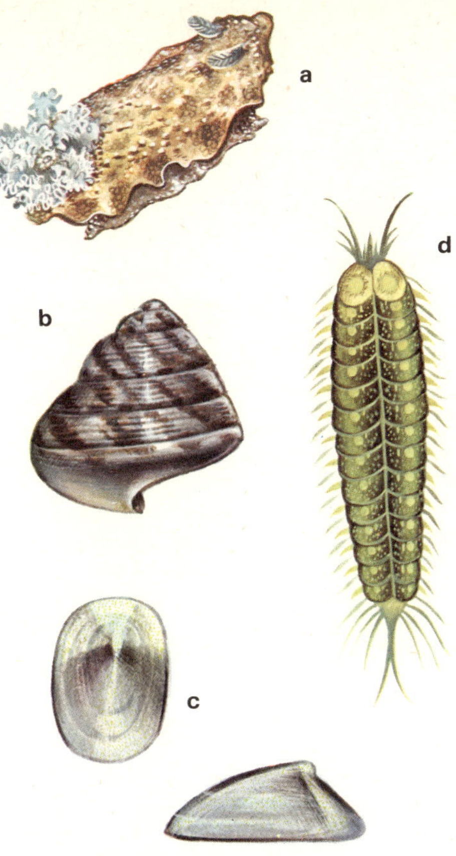

Above: The Sea Lemon (*a*) *Archidoris pseudoargus,* is a mollusc. It is a sea slug which feeds on the sponges and sea-anemones on the lower shore. The Grey Topshell (*b*) *Gibbula cineraria* is often abundant in this zone. The White Tortoiseshell Limpet (*c*) *Acmaea virginea* is found feeding on the *Laminaria* seaweeds and the scale-worm *Harmothoë impar* (*d*) can be found under stones. This is one of the swimming worms and grows to about $2\frac{1}{2}$cm long.

Right: The sponges on a rocky shore in cool waters are not as large as those found in warmer seas. They are fairly difficult to see, although they are often fairly brightly coloured. Some of them are found encrusting rocks and stones, such as (*a*) the Purse Sponge *Grantia compressa,* (*b*) *Leucosolenia coriacea,* the Breadcrumb Sponge, (*c*) *Halichondria bowerbanki* (*d*), *Adociacineria* (*shown magnified in* (*e*)), *Ophilitaspongia seriata* (*f*) and *Suberites domuncula* (*g*). The Slipper limpet shell (*Crepidula*) (*h*) has holes in it caused by one of the boring sponges *Cliona celata.*

sand and mud round the rocks as well as in the seaweeds. Some of the seaweed fronds and some of the rocks have little, coiled tubes on them, rather like tiny snails. These are made by worms, which keep tucked away inside them when the tide is out and come out to feed when they are surrounded by water again.

The animals found in the crevices of the rocks, or under large stones, are more difficult to find at first. It may be possible to see a flatworm gliding over the film of water left behind on a rock. The flatworms are dark coloured and very flat, which makes them difficult to find. The sea-squirts and sponges are easier to see and so are the cup corals. These animals stay in the same place all the time. They cannot move, so that when you have found one it is easy to find it again. It is interesting to visit animals found during low tide when there is water over them. Then it is possible to see them feeding. Sea-squirts look like little bags of jelly with some colours in them. They are called sea-squirts because they will squirt water over anything that treads on them. Sponges look like something squashed on to the rock. Cup corals look rather like sea-anemones in a cup. Like everything else on the beach, the only real way to know these animals is to see them for yourself.

THE SUB-LITTORAL ZONE

The sub-littoral zone is never uncovered when the tide goes out. It is the shallow part of the sea below the Spring tide low-water mark. It is the beginning of the sea proper. Although it is not strictly part of the beach, the sub-littoral community is affected by the beach, and its inhabitants are often washed up on the beach, or marooned in rock pools by the retreating tide. The shells of the sub-littoral molluscs are often washed ashore and taken home in triumph as trophies of a visit to the seaside. The best way to investigate the sub-littoral zone is with a mask and flippers. Swimming gently along like that, there is not too much disturbance and the animals are not unduly

Below: There are marine hydras, related to the well known freshwater ones. The two shown, *Coryne pusilla* (*left*) and *Tubularia indivisa* can be found on rocks in this zone and in pools higher up the beach.

Right: Three of the many red seaweeds to be found here: (*left*) *Delesseria sanguinea,* (*centre*) *Lomentaria clavellosa* and (*right*) Dulse, *Rhodymenia palmata,* which is edible.

alarmed. Wading stirs up the sea-floor so it is necessary to stand quite still for a while in order to watch the animals feeding.

The most noticeable seaweeds in this zone are the big brown seaweeds. There are great forests of kelp, oarweeds and tangles that sway gently about when the tide is in. The numerous fronds, looking like a strange, aquatic wood, provide shelter for a large number of fishes, swimming molluscs and other animals. The huge holdfasts, which can be as big as 30cm across, house small crabs, molluscs, worms and many other small animals. There is usually some sand or mud on the bottom, between the rocks, and starfishes and sea-urchins may be found there.

These seaweed forests do not continue right down into very deep water. The plants need sunlight in order to grow, and unless the water is very clear, the seaweeds cannot grow very far down. The water above rocks does not have as many tiny pieces of mud and sand suspended in it as the water above sand or mud would have, but it does have some. This helps to cut down the light reaching the seaweeds. Even in this region it is possible to see zones, because some seaweeds need less light than others, so they can grow deeper in the sea. Red seaweeds can grow quite a long way under the surface, as they can survive with small amounts of light. They also grow on the brown seaweeds. The oarweed that looks like giant, many-fingered hands needs quite a lot of light, and grows at the edge of the water. It is possible to paddle through this weed when the tide is out. The oarweed that is used to forecast the weather grows further out to sea, but it is often broken off during storms and

Below: *Laminaria saccharina* is an oarweed too. It is the one used to foretell the weather. The Gold-sinny Wrasse, *Ctenolabrus rupestris* is in the weed.

Below: The Common Whelk *Buccinum undatum* is common in this zone.

Left: The oarweed *Laminaria digitata* looks like giant hands under the water. The rock gobies *Gobius paganellus* swim about amid the plants.

Below: (*left*) *Goniodoris nodosa* is a prettily coloured sea slug found in this zone and in rock pools. The Grey Sea Slug (*centre*) *Aeolidia papillosa* can be found feeding on sea-anemones. The Sea squirt *Cliona intestinalis* (*right*) is found on rocks.

Above: One of the swimming worms, the bright green paddle-worm *Eulalia sanguinea,* is a meat-eating worm. It grows to about 5cm long, and can also be found under stones in the lower shore zone.

tossed up onto the beach. This is the seaweed with the very large holdfasts in which many animals shelter. The tangleweeds grow even deeper than all these.

The animals in the sub-littoral zone do not have to be as tough as the animals that live further up the beach, as they are never exposed to the sun and wind. The waves and storms disturb the zone to some extent, but not as violently as they do above the waves, and the animals can retreat into cracks in the rocks if the water gets too rough.

There are a great many different animals in this part of the beach. Both large and small crustaceans can be found, scuttling about on the sea-floor or hiding in the rocks. There are large numbers of worms living here, some of which are swimming worms, called paddle-worms. The sea-anemones decorate the rocks with their flower-like circles of tentacles. They wait for some unsuspecting swimming creature to come within reach of them. The anemones themselves have the Grey Sea Slug crawling about them, feeding on them.

In warmer seas the corals are found in the sub-littoral zone. Corals need a firm surface on which to start building their limestone skeletons. They also need warmth and reasonably shallow waters. The little coral animals, which are called polyps, slowly build up their great walls of lime, like blocks of flats. The sea inside these protective walls of coral is quiet, as the worst of the waves break outside them. The coral wall is called a reef. The corals build the reefs

Above: The sea-anemones are some of the loveliest animals on the beach. The ones shown here are (*a*) the Plumrose Anemone *Metridium senile*, (*b*) the Beadlet Anemone *Actinia equina*, (*c*) the Dahlia Anemone *Tealia felina*, (*d*) *Adamsia palliata*, the anemone which often grows on hermit crabs' shells, (*e*) *Sagartia elegans* and (*f*) the Snakelocks Anemone *Anemonia sulcata*.

Below: (*right*) The Squat Lobster, *Galathea squamifera* is often found in pools as well as tucked away into crevices in the rocks. The Shore Crab (*left*) is found on all types of shore, but the large ones are found near rocks. Its name is *Carcinus maenas*.

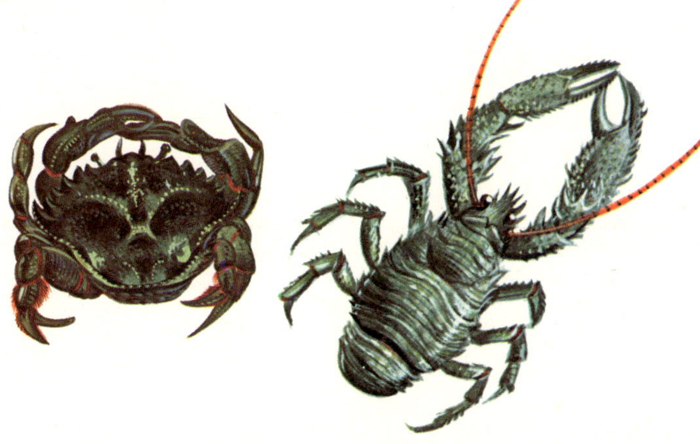

Below: This curious looking animal is the sea spider *Pycnogonum littorale* which is a parasite feeding on sea-anemones and soft corals.

up to the surface of the sea, but not into the air. Their food supply is in the sea and they cannot live where they cannot eat. In the quiet waters inside the reef there are a great many animals to be found. Hundreds of brightly coloured fishes, starfishes, sea-urchins, brain corals, swimming molluscs, gastropod molluscs, sponges and many other creatures live in the warm, peaceful waters. Delicate sea-anemones and jellyfishes can lead their sheltered lives away from the violent wave action.

Many molluscs live in the sub-littoral zone of a rocky beach. There are a number of the gastropod molluscs that browse on the seaweeds. The Common Whelk grows to a very large size in this zone, feeding on the plant-eating molluscs. Cowries, topshells, winkles and ormers are found in this region. Ormers are called abalones in America and paua shells in New Zealand. In the warmer seas of the world helmet

All the shells on this page are top-shells, from different parts of the world.

Above: *Zizyphinus zizyphinus*, the Painted Topshell, is found in the Mediterranean region, in British and Scandinavian seas.

shells, trumpet shells, conches and strombs are found. These shells are often very beautiful, and they are not too difficult to reach. Man uses a great many of them to decorate himself or, rather, women use them for trimmings and jewellery.

The helmet shell can be carved to make cameos. The outside of the shell is white, but there is a pink layer inside it. The white layer is carved away leaving, say, a head or bunch of flowers white against

a pinkish background. These little carvings are then made into earrings, bracelets, rings and necklaces.

The topshells are used to make pearl buttons. The topshells have a pearly layer covered by a brownish horny layer. The horny layer is removed and the pearly shell underneath is cut into discs to make buttons. Even the small topshells found washed up on the beach have often had the horny layer scraped off as they rolled about on the sand, so perfect little pearly shells can be found. The large topshells, which are found off the Japanese coast, were in danger of extinction not so long ago. They were saved when manufacturers began to make plastic

Above: The large shell is *Trochus niloticus* and it lives in the Indo-Pacific region (*shown in yellow on the map on page 14*). It is the shell that was once used to make pearl buttons. The smaller topshell is *Maurea tigris* and it is found in New Zealand.

Left: Not all the topshells have simple conical shells. These are also topshells. (*Left*) *Guildfordia yoka* is found in Japan. The other spiny shell (*top*) is *Angaria formosa*, like *Trochus niloticus* an inhabitant of the Indo-Pacific region. *Tristichotrochus formosensis* (*bottom*) is found in the deep water off the coasts of Taiwan.

Below: The ormers, abalones or paua shells are recognized by the row of holes in the shell. (*Top*) *Haliotus asinina,* (bottom) *Haliotus sanguinea.*

pearl buttons, which are easier to produce than the buttons made from seashells.

Apart from the molluscs that crawl about on the rocks, there are the swimming molluscs. These are the octopi and squids. They are related to the gastropods, but they have lost most of their shells. These molluscs swim about or wait beneath a rock for some animal to come within reach of their long tentacles. The octopus has only eight tentacles, while the squid has ten. The squids found in the sublittoral zone are quite small, but the ones that live far out to sea grow very large indeed, large enough to feed on small whales.

There are plenty of fishes swimming about in the forests of seaweeds, just as birds fly about between the trees in a wood. The wrasses, which feed on molluscs, are abundant. These delightful, brightly coloured fishes actually appear to turn on their sides and go to sleep at night. Rock-gobies, lumpsuckers, rocklings, blennies, shannies and gunnel fishes are also likely to be found here.

The animals and plants mentioned here are a very small proportion of the total population. The sublittoral zone is a very interesting place to search in and the best way of getting to know it is to search there yourself, armed with a key.

Above: The limpets are found all over the world. (*Left*) *Patinigera magellanica* lives in the same regions as the penguins. The ribbed limpet (*right*) is from the coasts of South Africa. They do not look quite the same, but they both browse on the rocks, feeding on Algae.

Far left: The Common Limpet *Patella vulgata,* is found in British and Scandinavian waters. Limpets have favourite resting places to which they return after crawling about. They actually wear away the rock because they clamp themselves to it so firmly.

Left: Another South African limpet *Cymbula compressa.*

ROCK POOLS

The rock pools are one of the best places on the sea-shore to see underwater life actually being lived. When the tide goes out it leaves behind animals that must protect themselves from the sun and the wind. In order to do this they clamp themselves against a rock, like a limpet, fold themselves up like a sea-anemone or crawl away into a crack or under some seaweed, and wait for the water to come back. They are not difficult to find, but they are not easy to see; they do not *do* anything. The rock pools are quite different. They are still covered with water. The

Below: The rock pools have many red seaweeds in them. *Griffithsia flosculosa* (*left*) and *Plumaria elegans* (*right*) both grow on the sides of the pools and on brown seaweeds growing in the pools.

Above left: (*Left*) *Chondrus crispus*, or Caragheen is one of the seaweeds that is used in the preparation of foods. It is used to make blancmanges gell. (*Right*) *Heterosiphonia plumosa*.

Left: Green seaweeds tend to be tolerant of fresh water and so are suitable inhabitants of rock pools. These four are fairly common.
(*a*) *Enteromorpha linza* is found in both brackish water and salt water.
(*b*) *Bryopsis plumosa* grows on the sides of pools. (*c*) *Cladophora rupestris* often grows beneath Bladder Wrack. (*d*) *Codium tomentosum* grows to about 30cm long and provides food for many marine animals.

animals can carry on with their feeding with no danger of drying up.

The best way to watch them is to find a comfortable rock beside a pool and to sit down on it. Make sure that no shadow falls across the pool to disturb the inhabitants and that you do not make any sudden movements. You will need a lot of patience.

The community in a pool is in no danger of drying up, but it has other problems. The sun beats down on the shallow water and it gets very warm. In cold weather it gets very cold, and may even freeze. In the summer, the sun warms up the water until some of it evaporates, leaving salt behind. By the end of six hours, the water may be very salty indeed. When

Below: Fishes are sometimes caught in pools by the tide. (*Bottom left*) the Common Goby *Gobius minutus*, (*bottom right*) the Bullhead *Cottus bubalis* and (*above*) the Butterfish *Pholis gunnellus*. The Butterfish is so named because it is slimy and very difficult to catch hold of.

Below: Copepods are often found in rock pools. These two species are very small, and a microscope or a strong hand lens are needed to see them. (*Left*) *Mesochra lilljeborgi* and (*right*) *Acartia clausi*.

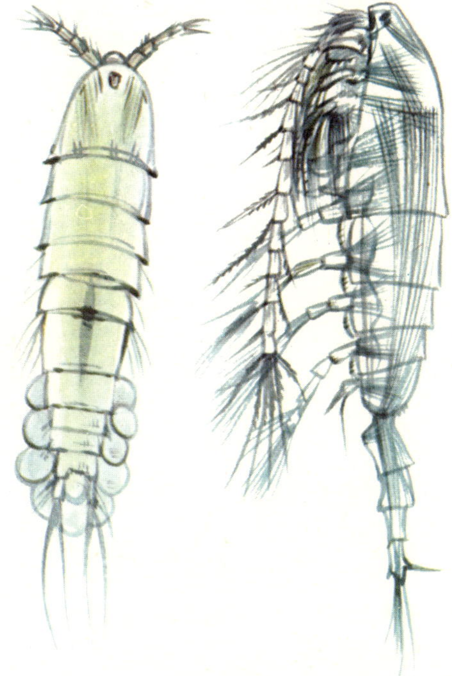

there is a rainstorm, the pool has fresh water poured into it. It gets less salty. The rock pool community has to be able to live in warm water and cold water; in very salty water and in almost fresh water. They have to be tough creatures.

There is a great variety of green, red and brown seaweeds in rock pools. These seaweeds do not usually grow very large, but they are often very thick. One red seaweed is very easy to recognize. It has a lime 'skeleton' and its colour ranges from deep pink to purple. It often deposits pink lime on the sides of the pool. It is named *Corallina*. There are many other seaweeds but it is better to look at them than to read a description of them. That is the only way to recognize each one.

Most rock pools have a little sand at the bottom. A large number of small crustaceans, such as Common Prawns, Chamaeleon Prawns and Skeleton

Right: This almost transparent little creature is a shrimp *Schistomysis spiritus,* which is often stranded in rock pools. It normally lives in deeper water, but it migrates towards the shore at night, and gets left behind by the tide.

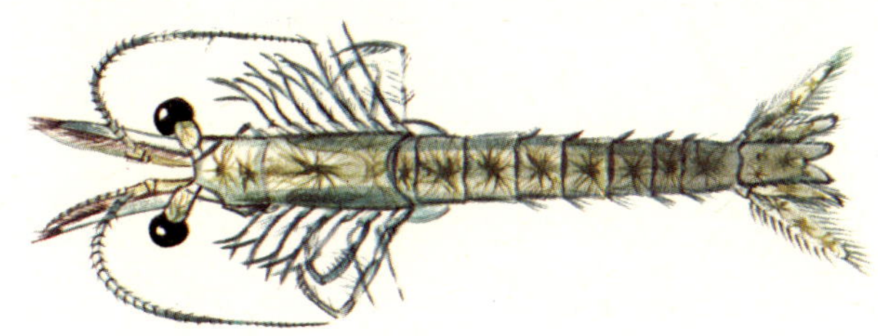

Left: The Hermit Crab *Pagurus bernhardus* is the largest of the British hermit crabs. That and the Aesop Prawn *Hippolyte varians* (*bottom right*) may be seen in pools. The Aesop Prawn is difficult to see because it changes colour to match its background. The flatworm *Procerodes littoralis* (*bottom left*) is found in pools with fresh water running into them.

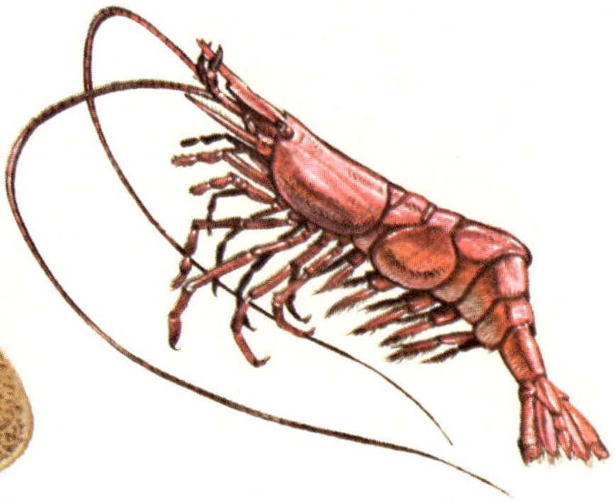

Above: The Edible Crab *Cancer pagurus* is found in pools occasionally. Only small specimens appear this far inshore, however, and only during the summer. In the winter the crabs go out to deeper water to spawn.

Below: Sea-anemones are an important animal in rock pool communities. The Beadlet Anemone *Actinia equina* (*top*) and the Dahlia Anemone *Tealia felina* (*bottom*) are both likely to be found there.

Prawns can be found in it. The sides of pools often have sea-anemones, such as the Beadlet Anemone and the Dahlia Anemone, living on them. If the sea-anemones are studied carefully, it may be possible to see the sea-spiders crawling about on their bodies. Cup corals are occasionally found in rock pools. They look rather like an anemone, but they have almost transparent tentacles and they sit in cups made of lime. The larger crustaceans, such as crabs, hermit crabs, squat lobsters and rock lobsters, may be marooned in a rock pool when the tide goes down. The hermit crabs would probably be wearing whelk shells. The crustacean that looks like a mollusc, the barnacle, may be seen feeding in a rock pool. The shells open at the top and long, feathery legs come out to sweep the waters for food. If there are barnacles, there is likely to be a dark green swimming worm there, feeding on them, and it may be possible to see flat worms gliding over the stones. Occasionally the delicate little brittlestars are left behind in a pool. They are related to the starfishes, but they are much more fragile.

SANDY BEACHES

UPPER SHORE

At first sight a sandy beach looks very empty. There are wide stretches of dry sand, with a line of dead seaweed and some empty shells on it. The splash zone and the upper shore zone do not look nearly as exciting as the same zones on a weed-strewn rocky beach. This is because seaweeds cannot grow in sand. They cannot put roots down into the earth as flowering plants can. They need a firm surface so that the holdfast can fasten itself to it to withstand the waves. If there are some large stones on the beach, there may be seaweeds growing on them, but there will not be any growing in the sand. So there is no thick seaweed shelter for the animals on a sandy beach.

The animals do shelter on sandy beaches, however. They do it by digging down into the sand. That is why the beach looks so empty at first glance.

A sandy beach is not a static beach. The wind has no effect on rocks, but it can blow sand about. The loose, dry sand is blown into sand dunes, and the sand dunes themselves are shifted backwards and forwards by the wind. If the wind and the tides move the sand in the same direction all the time, the beach can be blown into the sea. Man builds groynes on the beach to stop this happening. In some places in the world, the sand is blown inland and the beach covers forests and fields. Sand dunes are held firm by marram grass. This tough grass with long roots is often found on the sand dunes above high water mark. The roots spread through the sand so that it cannot shift about in the

Above: The high water mark usually has a line of dead seaweed to mark it. *Laminaria saccharina* often makes up a large part of this weed. The animals live in the decaying weed. The Seaweed Runner *Coelopa pilipes* can be found among them.

Left: The typical sandy beach looks empty, like this picture. The animals are all buried in the sand and no seaweeds can grow on sand. It does not look like a promising hunting ground at first sight, but this is not so; there is plenty to be found.

wind. Man plants marram grass on the dunes that threaten to overrun the land.

Below the dunes on a beach is the high water mark. This is shown by the line of dead seaweed left there by the tide. If you step on this seaweed, you are suddenly surrounded by a cloud of little hopping creatures. These are crustaceans and are aptly named sandhoppers. They are extremely good jumpers, and can jump several times their own length and height. They do this by suddenly straightening out their tails, which are normally bent under them. All the surface life in this zone is found in the dead seaweed at the high water mark. The other true seashore animal there is the Seaweed Runner. This is a small fly which is named after its habit of running over the seaweed when it is disturbed. Other insects, such as beetles, may be found in the seaweed, but they are land creatures that have stayed there.

There may be sea birds scavenging in the high water line but all the rest of the animals in this zone are buried deep down in the sand, where it is cool and damp. Even if you dug down to find the animals, you would need a microscope to see them.

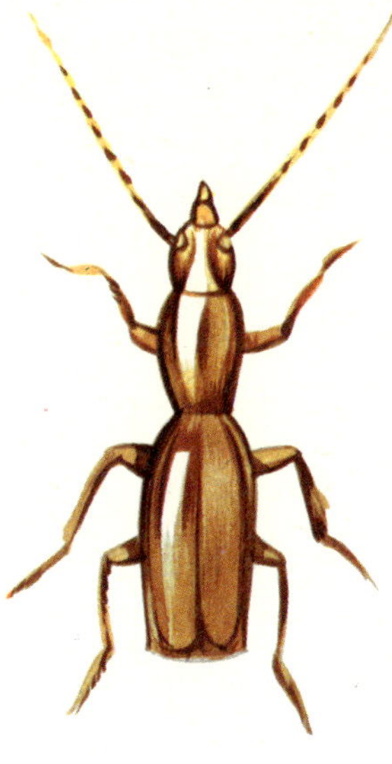

Above: There are a number of beetles found in the splash zone of a sandy beach. *Aepus marinus* is one of them. These small beetles are found under decaying seaweed.

Above: The Beach Flea *Orchestia gammarella* can be found in the rotting seaweed on both rocky and sandy shores. This animal is one of the few that are now almost land animals. They have succeeded in leaving the damp shores for the much dryer conditions inland, without becoming too dried up to survive.

Left: The Black-headed Gull *Larus ridibundus* sometimes nests in the dunes at the top of a sandy beach. It nests in colonies. The Black-headed Gull feeds on sea-shore animals, fishes and rubbish. It is found in Europe, Iceland and east as far as Asia. It migrates as far south as the Equator.

THE MIDDLE SHORE ZONE

The middle shore zone of a sandy beach does not have even the line of dead seaweed that can be seen in the upper shore zone of it. It looks much emptier than the higher zone. In fact there are plenty of animals living in this zone, but it takes a lot of digging to find them. The animals likely to be found on a sandy sea-shore come from three main groups. These are the molluscs, the worms and the echinoderms. Molluscs and worms have been met before. The echinoderms are the sea-urchins and starfishes. The molluscs are not like those found on the rocky shores. They have two shells instead of one. They are called bivalve molluscs. There are other groups of animals besides these three to be found on the shore, but these are the most obvious.

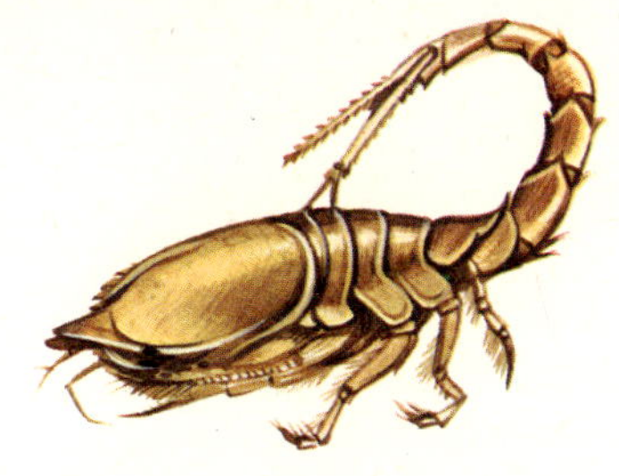

Above: There are many small animals buried in the sand to keep moist. This strange little beast is a crustacean named *Diastylis rathkii,* which may grow as long as one cm.

The problems that these animals face on a sandy shore when the tide is out are keeping moist, keeping cool and breathing. The top layers of the sand get very hot, but the layers underneath stay cool and moist, so the animals can solve the first two problems by burrowing deep into the sand. The breathing problem is more difficult. Aquatic animals normally breathe the oxygen that is dissolved in the water. They cannot use the oxygen in the air. When they bury themselves in the sand they use up the oxygen in the small amount of water round them fairly quickly. There is no more oxygen until the tide comes in again. Some of the animals store oxygen in their blood, and some slow themselves down so that they do not use very much. Scientists are studying these animals to discover how they manage to breathe.

Above: The tellins are typical sandy beach molluscs. With their two slim, highly polished shells, they are able to dig themselves into the sand quite quickly. These tellins are (*from left to right*); *Tellidora burneti,* which lives on the west coast of Central America; *Tellina foliacea,* from the Pacific shores; the Striped Sunset Shell, *Tellina virgata* from India and Asia; and *Tellina pulcherrima,* from the same area.

Below and right: This venus shell shows the structure of a bivalve mollusc. Its name is *Venus verrucosa.* The small tubes are siphons. The mollusc draws water in through one and blows it out through the other. In this way it breathes and feeds. It digs into the sand with its powerfully muscled foot, pulling the shells down after it. The soft parts of the body are well protected by the shell, which can enclose them completely.

The animals do not have to burrow only to keep damp and cool. They also have to escape the rush of water and the crash of the waves when the tide comes in again. The waves are likely to be carrying sand and pebbles with them, which could damage a fragile animal. The animals do not appear on the surface of the sand until the tide is some way in and the water is fairly deep.

The animals dig themselves in in different ways. The very small animals wriggle down between the grains of sand. The larger ones push the sand out of the way. Some of the worms push their way through the sand, others eat their way through. The bivalve molluscs dig with the help of the fleshy foot which is inside the two shells. When they want to dig themselves in, they push the foot down into the sand. Then they swell out the tip of the foot so that it grips the

Right: The sandy shore is the home of many worms, which dig themselves into the sand. Some of them are shown diagrammatically in this picture: (*a*) a rag-worm, *Nereis diversicolor,* which is a meat-eater; (*b*) the Cat-worm *Nephyths hombergi* is another; (*c*) *Syllis prolifera* may be found under stones on the sand. Many stones on a sandy beach have the little keeled tubes of *Pomatoceros triqueter* (*d*) on them, and the worm-casts and dimples (*e*) in the sand show where the lug-worm is burrowing. It is only possible to see the fans of the peacock-worms (*f*) when the tide is in. These are *Sabella pavonina.*

sand, and pull the shells down beneath the surface. The razor shells can dig themselves in so quickly that it is difficult to catch them, but cockles are slower.

Not all the animals on sandy shores move about. Some of them stay in one place and feed on the plankton in the water, and the bits of dead plant and animal on the surface of the sand. They are scavengers, and they help to keep the sand clean. Some of the worms make tubes from mucous from their bodies and grains of sand and live inside them. Some worms just dig burrows in the sand and line them to stop them collapsing. Some of the molluscs remain below the surface of the sand with just their siphons showing. The siphons are the tubes through which they feed and breathe.

The molluscs likely to be found on sandy shores in the middle shore zone are cockles, wedge-shells, clams and venus shells. It is necessary to dig fairly deep to find them. The worms buried in the sand are likely to be nemertines, nematodes, lug-worms and sand-masons. The worms swimming about when the tide comes in are most likely to be ragworms and white catworms. Apart from worms and molluscs there are little animals called copepods, many microscopic one-celled animals and some crustaceans related to the sand-hoppers. There is also a worm-like creature called an Acorn Worm, which is actually one of the links between the animals without backbones and the animals with backbones. It is a fragile worm and very difficult to collect.

Above: The Edible Cockle *Cerastoderma edule* (*top*) is excellent to eat. It is found in the middle and the lower shore zones of a sandy beach. The Soft Clam (*centre*) is also an important food, its name is *Mya arenaria*. The Acorn Worm *Saccoglossus cambrensis* (*bottom*) is about 6cm long. It is not a true worm, it is more nearly related to the animals with backbones.

THE LOWER SHORE ZONE

The sandy beach is not zoned as sharply as a rocky shore and many of the animals are found in both the middle and the lower shore zones. The groups of animals are the same in both zones. There are bivalve molluscs, worms and echinoderms. There are more echinoderms in the lower shore zone.

The invisible life in this zone is much richer than that further up the beach. There are protozoans, flatworms and the tiny crustaceans called copepods. They live in the gaps between the grains of sand and in the film of water round the grains. Most of them can only be seen with a microscope.

Some of the flatworms are most unusual. There is one that actually has plants growing inside it. It is a bright green colour. It feeds on the plants inside its body. The plants continue to grow and reproduce. To do this they need sunlight. The flatworm lives in the sand, and stays well below the surface of the sand when the tide is in. When the tide goes out, and there is no danger of the worm being washed away, the flatworm moves up to the surface of the sand. The plants inside it can then make food with the help of the sunlight. It is very interesting to watch this happen. At one moment there is a stretch of golden sand. Then, as if by magic, it turns green!

There are many more burrowing worms in the lower shore zone. Many of them live in tubes and put long, feathery tentacles out to feed when the tide

Above: The Rayed Trough Shell *Mactra corallina* can jump through the water. If it is put into a bowl of sea-water, it can be seen to do this. Both it and the otter shells *Lutraria lutraria* (*below*) are found buried in sand. The Common Otter Shell is usually about 60cm below the surface.

Left: The Razor Shell *Ensis arcuatus* (*right*) is a high speed digger. Once it starts to dig itself into the sand, it is very difficult to catch. (*Far left, top*) the Rayed Artemis, *Dosina exoleta*, (*centre*) the Cross Cut Carpet Shell *Venerupis decussata* and (*bottom*), the Faroe Sunset Shell, *Gari fervensis*. All three shells are typical of this zone of the beach.

: The rag-worm *Nereis virens* may be found under stones on the beach as well as in the sand. This worm can grow as long as 90cm.

comes in. Sand-masons, peacock-worms, tube-worms and lug-worms are found here. The lug-worms' burrows can be seen when the tide goes out. They are marked by worm casts at one end and dimples in the sand at the other end. Sandy shores are often covered with them at low tide. The flexible tubes made by the tube-worms often last after the worm has died, and can be found in the sand.

The other group of animals common in this zone is the echinoderms, the sea-urchins, starfishes, sea-cucumbers and brittlestars. The Heart Urchin buries itself in the sand and so does the sea-cucumber. The urchin digs itself in with its tube-feet and its spines. It is deep in the sand, eating sand and digesting any bits of plant or animal mixed up in it. Starfishes bury themselves just under the surface waiting for a mollusc to start feeding. Sea-cucumbers eat sand, taking it in with their tentacles.

Below: The sand-mason *Lanice conchilega* (*left*) makes a tube from mucous, grains of sand and bits of shell. *Polymnia nebulosa* (*right*) is another tube-builder. Both worms live in the lower shore zone. Both grow to about 30cm long.

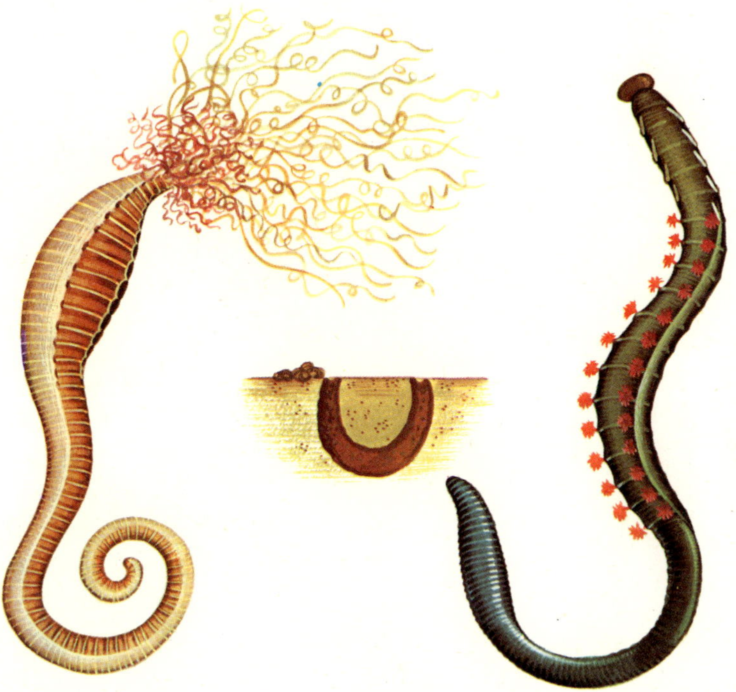

Left: Two more burrowers which are found in this region. The lug-worm *Arenicola marina* (*right*) is well known to fishermen as good bait. It builds a U shaped burrow (*centre*). *Amphitrite johnstoni* lines its burrow with mucous to hold up the sand grains.

THE SUB-LITTORAL ZONE

The sub-littoral zone is certainly the most exciting part of a sandy beach to look at. It is possible to see the animals, providing they are not alarmed by noise or splashing. The worms have their tentacles outside their burrows, sieving the water and the molluscs have their siphons sucking in water and debris from the surface of the sand. The cockles have a small spiky pair of siphons sticking up above the sand. The tellins have one small siphon and one long, snaky siphon, hunting about for food. The prawns will be shooting about on the sand, the starfishes will be hunting for unwary molluscs to eat and there may be some fishes swimming about. The sub-littoral zone does not look dead at all.

The bivalve molluscs found in this zone are likely to be cockles, clams, tellins, wedge-shells, gapers and razor shells. All these are burrowing molluscs. Scallops may be found on the surface of the sand and mussels attach themselves to any rock or groyne above the sandy sea-floor.

There are plenty of crustaceans in the sub-littoral zone. The crabs are represented by the Masked Crab. This small crab has a long, pointed front to its shell. When it is disturbed it sits itself up on its back legs and digs itself into the sand, back end first. Its long antennae and pointed shell are the last things to disappear. It leaves the tips of its antennae above the sand. There are many more burrowing crabs on tropical shores. Shore crabs are occasionally found in this zone and hermit crabs are often seen walking

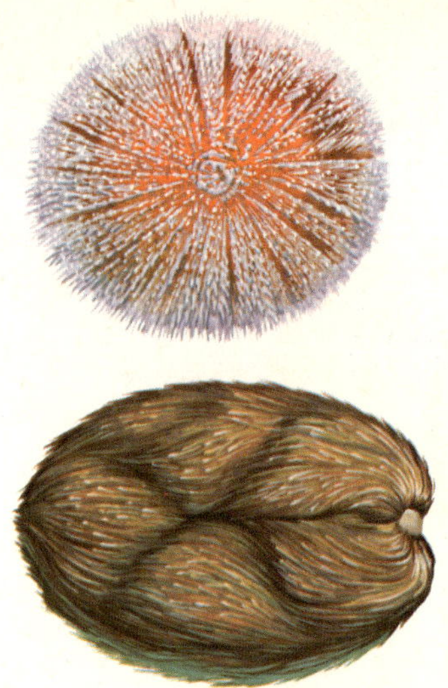

Above: The sea-urchins are found on sandy beaches, and are abundant in the sub-littoral zone. The Common Sea-urchin, *Echinus esculentus,* (*top*) feeds on algae and tube-worms. It is found near rocks as well as on sand. The Sea Potato, *Echinocardium cordatum,* also called the Heart Urchin, buries itself in the sand.

Below: (*Right*) the Common Starfish, *Asterias rubens,* is another echinoderm found on sandy shores. (*Centre*) the Masked Crab *Corystes cassivelaunus* is a burrowing crab. (*Left*) the Northern Quahog, *Mercenaria mercenaria,* is used as food and once made wampum.

about on the bottom. The other common crustaceans are the shrimps. These are often thick on the surface and just under the surface of the sand. Shrimping was once one of the great joys of a seaside holiday, and no-one went to the sea without a shrimping net.

Rag-worms and paddle-worms may be seen swimming about, hunting for food. These are active, meat-eating worms. The sea-mouse, which is a worm and not a mouse at all, may wander into this zone from the muddy shores.

The fishes are certainly not likely to be found in any other zone but this on a sandy beach. There are several fishes which live on sandy shores. The sand-gobies, the sand-eels and the weever fishes are all likely to be found. The sand-goby is very well camouflaged and is difficult to see when it is on the sea bed. Both sand-eels and weevers bury themselves in the sand. The weevers have a poisonous spine in the fins on their backs. It sticks up out of the sand when the fish is buried. The poison can make a man very ill if he steps on a spine. Both weevers and sand-eels eat shrimps.

Below: The Greater Sand Eel, *Ammodytes lanceolatus*, (*top*) and the Lesser Weever, *Trachinus vipera*, (*bottom*) are both likely to be found buried in the sand in the sub-littoral zone. The sand eel is about 20cm long and the weever about 15cm long.

Below: The scallops are bivalve molluscs that do not burrow into the sand. They live on the surface of the sand, and they are able to swim. They do this by quickly opening and closing their shells. They are found all over the world. The ones shown below are (*from top to bottom*) *Gloripallium pallium*, from India and Asia, *Chlamys sanguinolentus*, from the Red Sea and *Chlamys varia* from Britain and Scandinavia. The scallops are very good to eat.

MUDDY SHORES

The muddy shores are similar to the sandy shore in many ways. Many of the animals found buried in the sand may also be found buried in mud. Muddy shores often have small stones scattered over them with green seaweeds growing on them. This makes them more interesting to look at than the sandy shores. Muddy beaches are usually very flat which causes only very small waves. It is only in these peaceful conditions that mud can settle on the bottom. They are often near the outflow of a river. The beaches are so flat that there is usually very little zoning.

Muddy beaches have the only truly marine flowering plant growing on them. This is eel-grass. It provides shelter for many interesting animals and food for even more. Many birds come to feed on the

Below: Many of the worms found on sandy beaches are also found on muddy beaches. The lug-worm *Arenicola marina* (*top*) burrows in the sandy mud, but the numbers get fewer as the mud gets finer. The rag-worm *Nereis diversicolor* (*centre*) swims all over the beach, particularly in brackish water. The Honeycomb Worm *Sabellaria* (*bottom*) is found on rocks near muddy sand. This worm cements sand and shells together to make a solid tube. Some of these worms can build reefs.

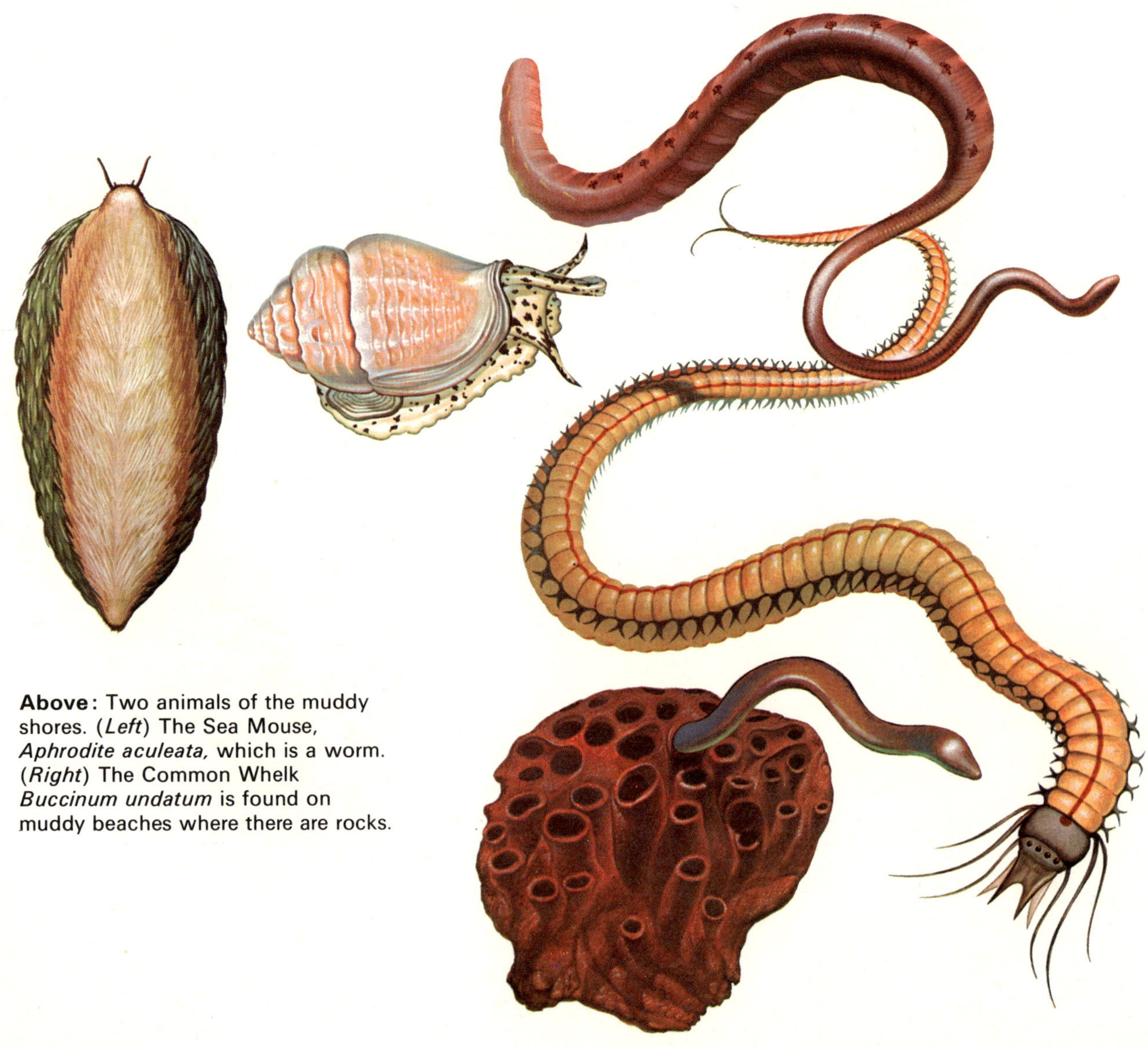

Above: Two animals of the muddy shores. (*Left*) The Sea Mouse, *Aphrodite aculeata,* which is a worm. (*Right*) The Common Whelk *Buccinum undatum* is found on muddy beaches where there are rocks.

grass or the animals sheltering there. Ducks, swans and geese feed there as well as waders of all kinds. Many snails are found crawling on the leaves, and the curious pipe-fishes live there.

There are many bivalve molluscs such as cockles, gapers and tellins buried in muddy beaches. The gapers grow very large and do not come out of their burrows, if they can avoid it. Small meat-eating whelks, like the Sting Whelk, feed on the bivalves.

The only burrowing sea-anemone lives on muddy beaches. It lives in a burrow. The burrowing worms, such as the peacock-worm, may be found here as well as the swimming worms. The sea-mouse is common on muddy shores. It is really a very pretty worm.

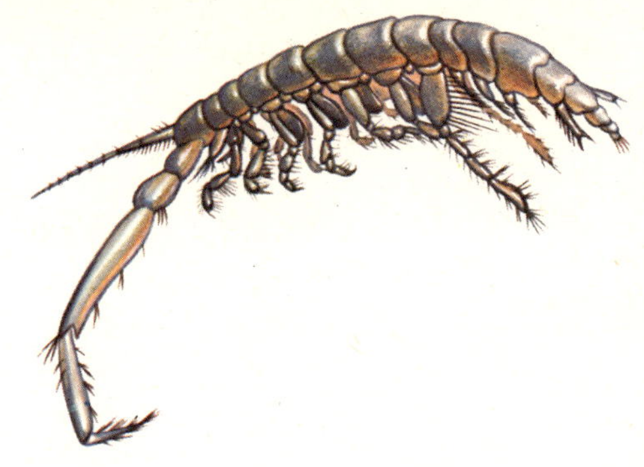

Above: This amphipod *Corophium volutator* digs burrows in the soft mud. It feeds on the bits of decaying plants and animals which fall to the muddy sea bed. It comes out of its burrow and crawls over the surface, feeding.

Above: The Sea Hare *Aplysia punctata* (*top*) is found feeding on Sea Lettuce, *Ulva lactuca* on stones on the muddy shore. The Netted Dog Whelk *Nassarius reticulatus* (*centre*) is a meat-eating mollusc. The Baltic Tellin *Macoma balthica* (*bottom*) is found in large numbers buried in the mud.

Left: The Red-necked Phalerope *Phaleropus lobatus* nests on marshy ground near water, and may be seen feeding on the beach. This bird is a wader, and feeds in the shallow waters over sandy and muddy beaches. It spins round on the water to stir up the edible animals in the sand or mud beneath it. It eats molluscs and worms.

ESTUARIES

Estuaries often have muddy shores, so many of the animals and plants already mentioned may be found in an estuary. The estuarine community has a great problem to overcome, however. When the tide is out, they are living in a river: when the tide is in, they are living in the sea. The plants and animals have to be able to live both in fresh water and in salt water, and the change from one type to the other takes place very quickly, twice a day. This mixture of salt water and fresh water is called brackish water.

The river water presents another problem. It brings fine particles of mud down from the fields. When these reach the salt water a lot of them stick together and sink to the bottom. Some continue to float in the water, however, and this floating mud cuts down the light shining through to the plants. The plants cannot make food without light, so they cannot live in muddy water. The animals that live by sieving food out of the water cannot live in muddy water, either. This is because the mud clogs their food-paths and the poor creatures starve. If the water in an estuary is muddy there are not many plants, or animals that live by sieving their food, in it.

Seaweeds grow in the brackish water of estuaries. The brown seaweed, Horned Wrack, attaches itself to rocks and piers. The bright green Intestine Weed and Sea-lettuce are found here too. Sea-lettuce is common on muddy shores. Eel-grass is another plant that grows in estuaries.

Below: The mussels are very tolerant of fresh water. The Common Mussel *Mytilus edulis* (*top*) is often found on rocks in estuaries. The Horse Mussel *Modiolus modiolus* (*bottom*) is found in muddy gravel. The Pea Crab *Pinnotheres pisum* is always found inside the Common Mussel.

Above: The Common Sand Gaper *Mya arenaria* is a large burrowing mollusc. It may grow as long as 15cm. It is abundant in estuaries, where it burrows into the sand. It is taken for food in some places, and is then called a clam.

Above: The Sea Trout *Salmo trutta*
may be seen swimming through the
estuary on its way upstream to
spawn. This picture shows the male
(*top*) and the female (*bottom*). The
eggs hatch upstream and after some
months the young smolt come downstream to the sea.

There are three kinds of animals found in estuaries. There may be some freshwater animals that have been swept downriver into the estuary by the current. There may be some marine animals that have swum in from the sea and there will be some animals that live there for all or for most of their lives.

There are some crustaceans which are permanent members of the estuarine community. One is a small creature closely related to the sand-hoppers. It is named *Gammarus* and there is a freshwater *Gammarus* and a marine one as well as the estuarine one. They are often called shrimps. There are also two types of prawn found in brackish waters.

There are both bivalve molluscs and gastropod molluscs living in this region. Some of the bivalve molluscs are burrowing molluscs like the gapers and the clams. The other type of bivalve mollusc cements itself to rocks, piers or some other suitable firm surface. Mussels and oysters are both found in estuaries. There are not many 'wild' oysters now. Man cultivates them because they are so delicious to eat. They were well-known in Roman times and were probably eaten before that. This Edible Oyster should not be confused with the Pearl Oyster, which grows in warmer seas. Pearls are occasionally found in the Edible Oyster, but it is valuable enough as a food without having to supply jewels as well!

Besides the bivalve molluscs, there is a small gastropod mollusc found in large quantities on the mud flats of estuaries. It feeds on Sea-lettuce and on the debris in the mud. When the tide goes out, the animal burrows into the mud. When the water comes back, the mollusc comes to the surface, makes a raft

Above: The Flounder *Pleuronectes flesus* lives in the estuary for most of its life. It can live in salt water and in almost fresh water. The Flounder feeds on cockles and tellins.

Left: There are three species of eel in estuaries. This is the Common Eel, *Anguilla anguilla* which swims through the estuary on its way to the Sargasso Sea to breed. The eel can live in salt water and fresh water and even crosses wet fields to reach ponds and lakes.

of bubbles and floats inshore with the tide. It rides on the bottom of its raft. When the tide turns, the mollusc drifts back out until it reaches the part of the shore it started from. It then drops to the bottom and browses until it is time to bury itself again.

Many fishes are found living in estuaries or passing through them. The Three Spined Stickleback is an estuarine fish, and flounders are often found there. Salmon and trout pass through on their way upriver to lay their eggs. The eggs hatch and two years later the young fishes swim through the estuaries on their way to the sea. The Common Eel lives part of its life in rivers and part in the sea. It does it the opposite way round from the salmon and trout. It is hatched at sea, miles away in the Pacific Ocean and swims and drifts back across the sea to Europe, where it swims upriver to live. After some years it swims downriver again, and back across the ocean to lay its eggs.

Conger Eels, Moray Eels, and many other sea fishes, like Sea Perch, Pollack and Grey Mullet may be found in the estuary.

Above: The Daisy Anemone *Cereus pedunculatus* is one of the few anemones which does not live on a rocky shore. It attaches itself to stones beneath the surface of the sand or mud.

Far left: *Gammarus* is a shrimp-like creature which is abundant in brackish waters.

Left: *Hydrobia ulvae* is the small mollusc that floats on a raft of bubbles on the incoming tide. It is just under one cm in length, and it may be so abundant that it covers the surface of the mud like gravel.

GROYNES, PIERS AND ROCKS

Many animals are found inhabiting the man-made structures on the seashore. Some fasten themselves to the outside and some burrow into them. It is worth looking hard at these places.

The most obvious animals are the mussels. These bivalve molluscs anchor themselves to firm surfaces by fine threads, called byssus. Mussels are very good to eat, but they must be kept alive in clean water before they are cooked as some of the things they eat are poisonous to Man, and have to be cleared out. The Goose Barnacles are easy to see. They often grow on wooden piers.

Many of the animals that live here live inside the structures. There are wood and rock boring molluscs, worms and crustaceans. The holes made in wood are probably made by the Gribble. This little crustacean causes a great deal of damage. Shipworms are as destructive. They used to damage the wooden planking in ships, but now they break down groynes. Despite its name the shipworm is a mollusc. The Piddock is a rock-boring mollusc which grinds its way into pier supports and ordinary seashore rocks. There may be sea-urchins, worms and sponges in burrows in the rocks as well, if you look hard enough.

Above: The Goose Barnacle *Lepas anatifera* can be found on wooden piers. It also grows on the bottom of ships.

Below: (*Left*) The Shipworm *Teredo navalis.* (*Right, top*) The White Piddock *Barnea candida.* (*Right, bottom*) The damage to timber caused by *Teredo.*

Above: The Gribble (*left*) burrows into wood making it dangerously weak. The Gribble's scientific name is *Limnoria lignorum.* (*Right*) Wood damaged by the Gribble.

Left: Jetties and piers are often covered by thick clusters of the Common Mussel, *Mytilus edulis.* These mussels can be collected, cleaned and eaten.

ANIMALS THAT FLOAT NEAR THE SHORE

Very early in the morning, when the Sun is still low on the horizon, it is possible to go to the end of a pier or jetty and see a very beautiful sight. On a clear summer morning, with the sky pale blue overhead, the sea is a clear, bright blue. Just under the surface of the water the light catches millions of tiny animals that sparkle and glitter like underwater stars. There is a rainbow flash here and there as the sunlight catches a sea-gooseberry. The whole thing is quite breath-taking. The animals can be collected by simply

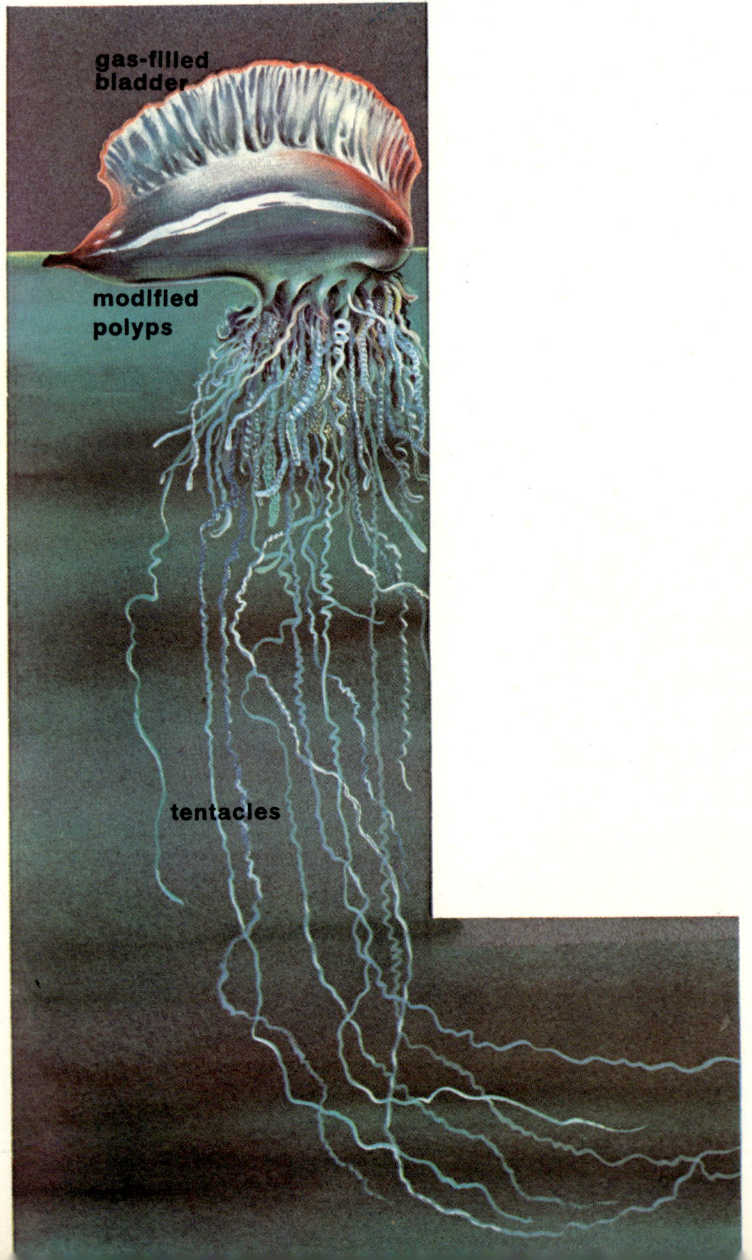

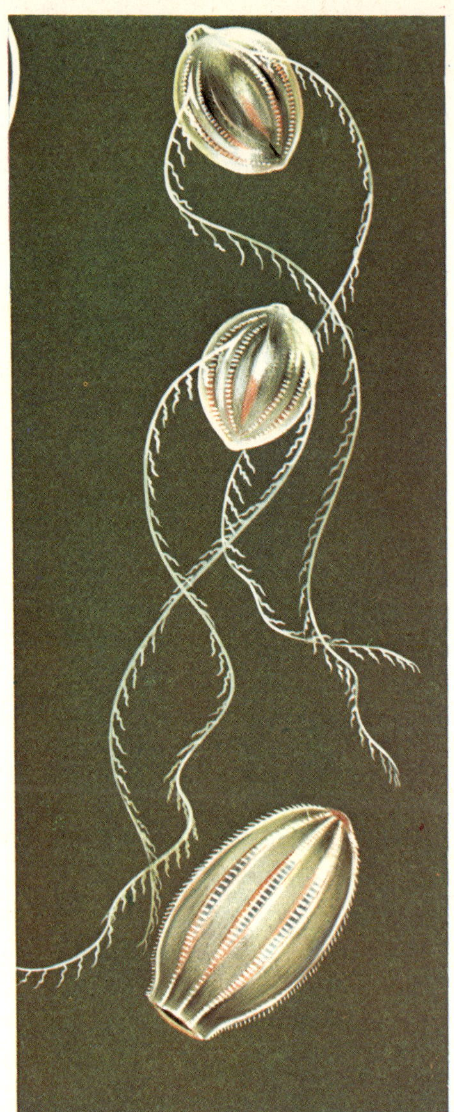

Above: The Sea Gooseberries, or Comb-jellies, drift about in the off-shore plankton. They move the combs which are in rows down their sides, by which means they can swim a little. The species shown here are (*top*) *Pleurobrachia pileus* and (*bottom*) *Beroë cucumis*.

Left: The Portuguese Man-o-War, *Physalia physalia* floats along on the top of the sea, blown by the wind. This lovely jellyfish has a nasty sting, and should not be touched if it is washed up on a beach.

dipping a jam-jar into the sea. This sight only lasts for a few minutes. As the Sun rises higher in the sky, the light gets too strong for the drifting animals and they sink down deeper into the sea.

The animals left in the jam-jar are part of the plankton which is found drifting in the surface layers of the oceans over most of the world. There are usually copepods, various larvae and jellyfishes and sea-gooseberries. The jellyfishes are large enough to see fairly well without a microscope. They are very beautiful animals, usually semi-transparent and delicately coloured. Many of them are umbrella shaped. They are related to the sea-anemones, and have life histories as complicated as a butterfly's, and pass some time in a form rather like a sea-anemone. Jellyfishes, like sea-anemones, have stings in their tentacles. They catch their food by stinging it until it is paralysed and then drawing it into their mouths. Some of them have stings which are powerful enough to harm Man. They usually drift through the water, but they can swim after a fashion by opening and shutting their umbrella-like bodies. Some of them live underwater and some drift on the surface. The Common Jellyfish is an underwater one and the Portuguese Man-o-War and the Sailor-by-the-Wind are surface dwellers.

The sea-gooseberries, or comb-jellies, are small, round, semi-transparent creatures. They have rows of combs down the sides of their bodies which reflect rainbow colours as they move. They are very pretty.

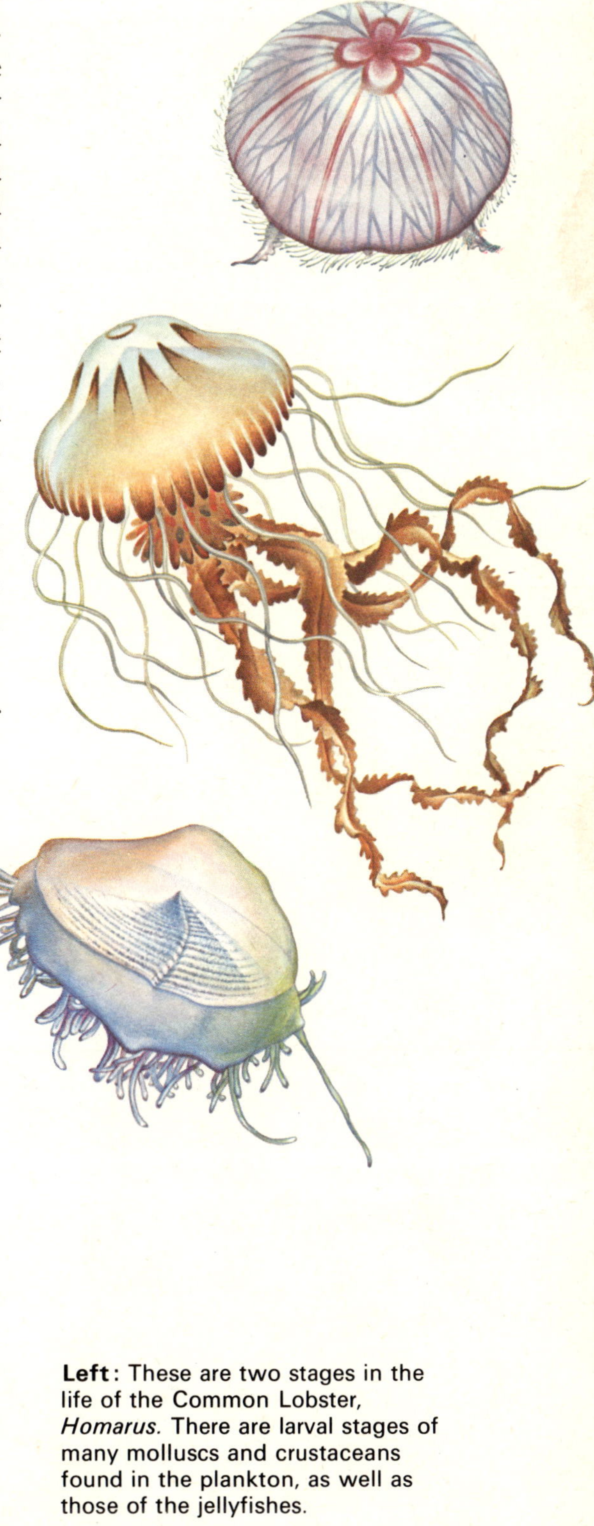

Below: The Common Jellyfish *Aurelia aurita* (*top*) drifts about underwater, and so does *Chrysaora isosceles,* (*centre*). The Sailor-by-the-Wind, *Velella spirans* (*bottom*) is a surface drifter, like the Portuguese Man-o-War.

Left: These are two stages in the life of the Common Lobster, *Homarus.* There are larval stages of many molluscs and crustaceans found in the plankton, as well as those of the jellyfishes.

ANIMALS THAT SWIM NEAR THE SHORE

Above: The Velvet Swimming Crab, *Macropipus puber* has its shell covered with dense hair. It swims about near rocks and weeds, and may be found sheltering under the weed when the tide is out. It grows to about 10cm.

The warm, shallow seas near the coasts are crowded with life, so much so that it is only possible to mention a little here. There are large numbers of fishes swimming about in this food-rich area as well as molluscs and crustaceans. In some parts of the world it is possible to see this life through the glass bottom of a boat.

Some of the fishes have already been mentioned because they can be seen in pools near the shore. Some of the fishes are too big to come so far inland that they are caught by the tide. Dogfishes swim round the rocks on some shores, and flatfishes such as plaice, dab, sole and flounders live on the sea-floor. Young cod are often found near the shore, in fairly shallow waters, at times.

The swimming molluscs, the octopi and squids, are not easy to see until they are startled, when they shoot away by jet propulsion. There are also crabs that swim about near the shore. In warmer seas the sea-turtles swim ashore to lay their eggs in the sand.

Below: The dogfishes are small relations of the sharks. The Tope *Galeus vulgaris* (*far left*) is one of the larger dogfish. The Lesser Spotted Dogfish *Scyllium canicula* (*right*) is smaller, about 60cm long.

Above: The octopus *Octopus vulgaris* is a swimming mollusc found in the crevices of rocks. It is stranded occasionally in pools. The animal shoots through the sea by forcing water out through its siphon. It does not grow much larger than 25cm long. The octopi in warmer waters grow much larger.

MAMMALS ON THE SEASHORE

The commonest mammal to be seen on the seashore these days is Man. There are others, however, on quieter beaches, and it is still possible to see some of them. The seals, sea-lions and walruses live in the sea for most of the year, but they come ashore to breed. Seals can often be seen round the coasts of islands in ones or twos, but at breeding time they congregate in hundreds, crowding the beaches so that it is difficult to walk between them. They usually live in cool waters. The sea-lions are found all over the world. They are intelligent animals and are often trained and used in circuses. The walrus lives in the icy Arctic, and cannot strictly be said to 'come ashore' at all. More often than not it crawls on to ice, and never touches land as we think of it.

In warmer waters the mammals are represented by the sea-cows. These are the animals that gave rise to the mermaid legends. Sailors described them as beautiful maidens with tails. One glance at a sea-cow is enough to shatter this romantic story. They are most certainly not beautiful.

The most playful and entertaining of the seashore mammals is the sea-otter. This delightful creature looks rather like its inland relative. It is very rare now because it has the misfortune to have a beautiful, thick fur and was hunted to the point of extinction in the past.

The porpoises and dolphins do not actually come up on to the beach, but they do come in near the shore. They are extremely intelligent mammals that look like fishes. They are magnificent swimmers.

Above: The Walrus *Odobenus rosmarus* lives in the Arctic. Both the male and the female Walrus have long tusks, which they use to dig up their food. They eat bottom living molluscs. The Walrus grows to about 360cm in length.

Right: The Grey Seal *Halichoerus grypus* is often seen on rocky shores. It feeds on fishes, which it catches underwater. The seals gather in colonies to breed, and can be seen from the shore fairly easily. They are inquisitive animals and may come near to see what is going on. They live in the North Atlantic.

OFFSHORE BOTTOM DWELLERS

The seashore does not, of course, stop abruptly at the sub-littoral zone. The sea bed continues to slope gently away from the land for some distance. This wide, gentle slope is called the continental shelf. At the edge of the shelf there is a steep underwater cliff which drops down to the deeper, darker parts of the sea. The whole of the continental shelf is rich with life. Seaweeds continue to grow as long as there is enough sunlight shining through the water to help them to make their food. Even when the water is too deep for seaweeds, there are still molluscs, sponges and echinoderms living on the sea-floor. Sometimes their shells are washed up on the seashore after a storm. They are eagerly sought after by shell collectors. These animals are very rarely seen alive on the shore. It is only possible to see them with skin-diving equipment.

Sponges are found all over the world. They are animals, despite their plant-like appearance. They are animals that stay in the same place all their lives, usually fastened to a rocky bed. The sponge is not usually one animal, but a colony of many joined together. They feed by drawing a current of water through their bodies and filtering out the plankton. Large sponges are found in warm waters of the world.

The large and colourful corals are found in the warm parts of the world. Corals have already been mentioned in the sub-littoral zone of a rocky beach.

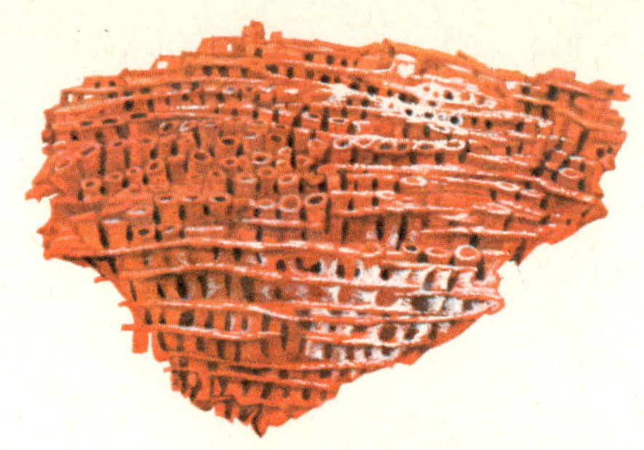

Above: (*Top*) The Organpipe Coral *Tubipora musica* is one of the reef-building corals. It grows in the warm waters, and is important in the building of coral rocks. (*Bottom*) The Honeycomb Sponge, or Bath Sponge *Hippiospongia equina* lives in the Mediterranean Sea.

Below left: The coral reefs grow in warm, shallow waters. This picture shows an island surrounded by a reef. The sea between the island and the reef would have many animals living in it.

Below: The Green Snail *Turbo marmoratus* is found near rocks. It is the largest turban shell.

They are not found in very deep waters, but solitary corals grow on the continental shelves in cool seas and the reef corals are found in warmer waters.

The echinoderms are true sea-floor animals. Echinoderms and sponges are found on the bed of the sea in the deepest parts of the oceans. They are abundant in the coastal waters. There are five different types of echinoderm. They are the starfishes, the sea-urchins, the sea-cucumbers, the brittlestars and the lovely featherstars. It is possible to see the first four groups alive on the shore, but the featherstars very rarely come ashore. They are collected by trawling for them. Starfishes and sea-urchins walk about on the sea-floor on their tube feet. Some sea-urchins walk about on the tips of their long spines, looking as though they are on stilts. The starfishes

Right: (*Top*) the murex shells are meat-eating gastropod molluscs. They feed on bivalve molluscs. This animal is *Poirieria zealandia* and it lives off the coasts of New Zealand. The murex put their spines between the bivalve's shells to stop them from closing.

Centre: The echinoderms are common offshore bottom dwellers. These are, (*from top to bottom*) the Common Sunstar, *Solaster papposus,* a brittlestar, *Amphipholis squamata*, the Common Starfish *Asterias rubens* and the Spiny Starfish *Marthasterias glacialis.* These starfishes often lose an arm under a rock or to an enemy, but they can grow another quite easily. They are not often seen alive on the beach, as they normally live out in the shallow water.

Below: A starfish opening a clam by pulling apart its shells. It then turns its stomach inside out, into the middle of the clam, and eats it.

show great patience when it comes to feeding. They feed on bivalve molluscs. The molluscs pull their two shells together and hold them with a strong muscle. The starfishes wrap themselves round the mollusc and pull steadily. They go on pulling until the muscle holding the shells together grows tired, and the shells open. Then the starfish eats the mollusc.

The molluscs are probably the most beautiful of the community living on the continental shelf. The bivalve molluscs like the scallops are fairly attractive to look at, but the gastropod molluscs produce the most graceful, gaily coloured shells. The ones living in the warm waters of the Indian and Pacific Oceans are the most beautiful of all. The shells are very elegant and are decorated with whirls and spines.

Man uses these shells in many different ways. He may well first eat the contents. The shells are then used as money, as containers and as trumpets. There

Above: The molluscs' shells are often very beautiful shapes. This turrid, *Thatcheria mirabilis* is a graceful shell that lives off the coast of Japan. It has a poisonous spine which it can use as a weapon.

Right: All the cowrie shells are beautiful. These few give some idea of the sizes and colours. The shells are very shiny. (*a*) *Cypraea argus* is 8cm long. (*b*) *Cypraea stolida* is about 2½cm long. (*c*) *Cypraea ziczac* is 2cm. (*d*) The Money Cowrie *Cypraea moneta* is 2½cms. (*e*) *Cypraea carneola* is 5cm and (*f*) the Humpback Cowrie *Cypraea mauritiana* is 9cm. The African mask is decorated with Money Cowrie shells.

Below: The Frilled Venus *Bassina disjecta,* a collectors prize.

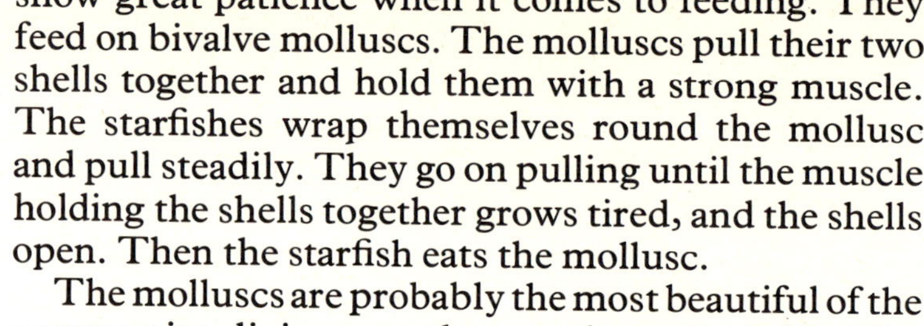

are two molluscs that have been used as money. One is the little Money Cowrie, which was used as money over a large part of the world until fairly recently. The other is a bivalve, the quahog, which the North American Indians used to make wampum. Many different gastropod shells are used as trumpets. The trumpet-shells and the conches are probably the best known. Many of the large gastropods make suitable water-carriers. The huge false trumpets are used by the Australian aborigines. The molluscs can claim to have the largest members of the animals without backbones in their family. These are the squids, which live out at sea and the Giant Clams which are offshore bottom dwellers. These huge bivalve molluscs may have a shell as long as 135cm and weigh as much as 263kg.

There are many other groups of animals found in this region. The acorn-worms and sea-squirts are much larger than they are nearer the beach. There are burrowing worms found in the sand, with their tentacles spread out, feeding on the debris on the surface of the sand. Crustaceans such as prawns also feed on the decaying plants and animals which sink down from the top layers of the water. The demersal fishes, the bottom feeders, move about the sea bed.

Above: The volutes are gastropod molluscs that feed on other molluscs. These are (*from top to bottom*) *Ampulla priamus,* from Spain and Portugal; *Lyria anna,* from India and Asia; and *Iredalina aurantia* from New Zealand.

Left: The Pacific Triton *Charonia tritonis* is used as a trumpet in the Pacific Islands. A hole is bored into the spine and a bamboo cane put into it.

SEABIRDS

SEABIRDS THAT NEST ON CLIFFS

The most noticeable, and the noisiest of all the inhabitants of the seashore are the birds. The word seaside conjures up a picture of wheeling, screaming gulls, darting terns, diving cormorants and dignified waders. The noisiest part of the shore is where the birds build their nests. Many of these birds choose to nest on cliff faces.

Many seabirds nest in colonies. You very rarely find just one or two nests. You are more likely to find dozens, or on quiet offshore islands, hundreds. It is not difficult to see where these birds choose to nest. The cliff face is usually white with the birds' droppings, and the noise is deafening.

Birds which lay their eggs on cliffs do not always build nests. They may gather a few pieces of dry seaweed, and sticks together. Guillemots, razor-bills, gulls, kittiwakes, fulmars, cormorants and shags are

Above: The Shag, *Phalacrocorax aristotelis* nests in colonies or by itself on small ledges on the cliffs. It builds a nest from seaweed. It also nests in caves and cracks in the rocks. Shags and their relatives the cormorants are found all over the world.

Left: The guillemots nest in colonies on the cliffs. They do not build a nest, but lay their single eggs on the bare rock. The Common Guillemot *Uria aalge* spends quite a long time on the cliffs. The other two shown here are (*bottom left*) Brunnich's Guillemot *Uria lomvia* and (*bottom right*) the bridled form of the Common Guillemot.

all found nesting on cliffs. They make use of ledges of rock. Guillemots just lay the egg on a suitable ledge. Gulls make untidy nests while gannets and cormorants make very bulky nests. A gannet's nest may be 60cm high.

Some birds lay their eggs in burrows in the soil on cliffs. Puffins, petrels, whale-birds and auklets all live in burrows. Some birds take over rabbit burrows and some dig their own. Storm petrels dig their own burrows. The birds usually enter and leave the burrows at dawn or dusk. They may spend the day inside the burrow, or feeding at sea.

Above: The Fulmar *Fulmaris glacialis* breeds in colonies on cliffs. It makes little or no nest, and lays one or two white eggs. The fulmar chick has an excellent method of defence. It regurgitates an oily liquid all over any attacker. The liquid is very smelly.

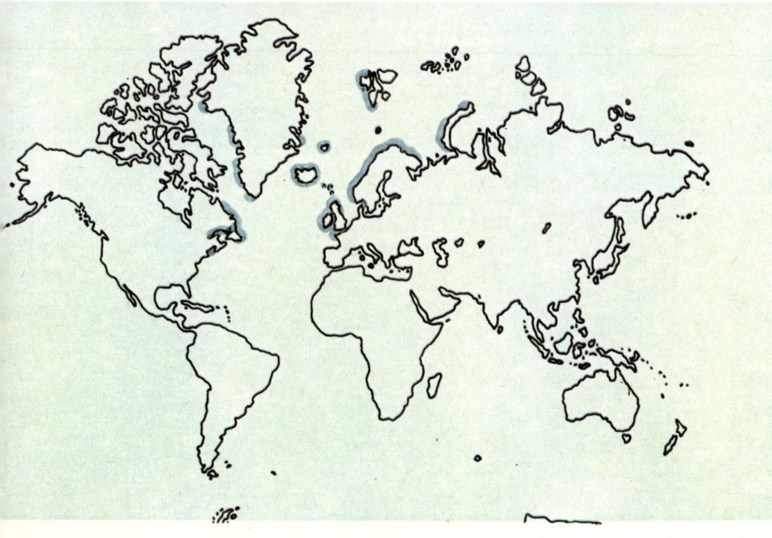

Left: The Atlantic Puffin, *Fratercula arctica* is a delightful bird that looks as if it is wearing clown's make-up. It nests in burrows on the steep slopes above cliffs. It lays one egg. The puffin may dig its own burrow, or take over a rabbit burrow. The map shows the parts of the world in which this puffin lives. It lives near the cool seas. The puffins are not very good fliers. They need a long stretch of water in order to take off. They run, with their wings flapping and their feet slapping the water, for a long way before they are moving fast enough to take off.

SEABIRDS THAT NEST ON MOORS AND MARSHES

Many of the seabirds nest amid the tussocks of grass and in the loose soil of moors near the sea. Many of the waders make their nests in the damp surroundings of a marsh. Some of the gulls have adapted themselves so well to the life on the moors that they do not go to the sea at all. They nest on the inland moors and feed on rubbish dumps, and from household scraps.

Gulls are very versatile birds. They can live in all sorts of different places. Their nests may be found on dunes, in grassy tufts, on floating vegetation and on cliffs. Their tastes in food are as wide as their nesting sites. They will scavenge for scraps, follow a fishing

Below: The Arctic Skuas *Stercorarius parasiticus* build their nests in a dip in the ground, lining it with grass and stems. They may breed in colonies, or by themselves. They lay two or three eggs, which are olive-brown and brown spotted. The birds shown show the different colours of the Arctic Skua, which can be dark or light.

fleet and feed on the offal tossed overboard when the fishes are cleaned, and entertain the holidaymaker by swooping down to catch scraps flung into the air for them. They will also hunt and eat chicks of other birds and fish for their food. The Great Black-backed Gull is a hunter. It feeds on rabbits, shearwaters, puffins, other seabird chicks, meat bones and scraps and fish.

Terns are related to gulls and are similar in colouring. They are called sea-swallows because of their long, pointed wings and their forked tails. Terns nest on moors, marshes, dunes and in shingle. The nests may be a simple hollow in the ground, or the hollow may be lined. Terns eat fishes, which they dive to catch. They also eat insects, molluscs, crustaceans and worms. Terns live all over the world.

The skuas are the pirates and brigands of the bird world. They are large birds, which scrape a hollow in the earth in which to lay their eggs. The adult birds often stand sentinel on tufts of grass near the nest.

64

Right: The skuas are pirates, chasing other birds to make them disgorge their food. This Great Skua *Catharacta skua* is chasing a Kittiwake *Rissa tridactyla.* The Great Skua is another moor nesting bird, laying eggs in a nest scraped in the ground and lined with grass.

Skuas are thieves. They can feed themselves if there are no other birds about, but if there is another bird about, the skua does not bother to go and search for itself. It chases gulls, fulmars, gannets, terns and Great Shearwaters and harries them until they disgorge their food. The skua catches the food in mid-air, and flies off after another bird. Skuas have an alarming way of protecting their nests. If the nest is approached too closely, the skua comes swooping out of the sky and strikes the intruder on the head with its feet. The skua is a large, heavy bird and can hit its opponent very hard.

Left: The Black-backed Gull *Larus marinus,* is an adaptable bird, able to nest anywhere suitable. It nests both on moors and on cliffs. It is a hunting gull, with a large appetite. It lays two or three eggs in a nest made from stems or seaweed.

The wading birds are important members of the sandy and muddy shore communities. As their name suggests, they wade about in the shallow waters, feeding on the molluscs and worms that come up when the tide comes in. Oystercatchers, avocets, lapwings, plovers, greenshanks, redshanks, sand-pipers, sanderlings, dunlins and phaleropes are a few of the birds likely to be seen on sandy or muddy shores.

Left: The Herring Gull *Larus argentatus* is a scavenger, feeding on a variety of foods. When it cannot feed on the scraps discarded by Man, it eats fishes, crustaceans, molluscs, insects, small mammals and birds. It probes in the sand with its beak and stamps on the sand to make worms come to the surface. Like the Black-backed Gull, it is adaptable, and nests in a variety of places, including islands in lakes. It nests in colonies and makes a well lined nest. It lays two to five olive-brown eggs. Herring Gulls have been studied very carefully by scientists to find out how they behave. The red spot on their bottom bill is very important. If it were not there, the chicks would not peck at it, and the parents would never feed the chicks. The chick pecking at its bill is the trigger to make the gull feed the chick. Chicks will peck at pieces of wood with a red spot on them.

Left: The Common Gull *Larus canus* is found all round the Northern Hemisphere. It nests in colonies on moors and bogs as well as rocky islands. It builds its nest with grass or stems. The Common Gull's diet is similar to that of the Herring Gull. The gulls find airports rather similar to the moors, being flat and grassy, and they cause some damage to aeroplanes by colliding with them at take-off or landing.

Many of these birds nest on marshy ground, nesting in floating vegetation. Some scrape a hollow in dry ground.

The eggs of all these birds are usually camouflaged, so that they are difficult to see at first glance. They are usually a buff, greenish or greyish colour, speckled with darker blodges. The adults do not often leave the nests unattended, but when they do the nests are not all that easy to find. The chicks are usually well disguised at first.

The shearwaters burrow into the grassy, treeless tops of rocky islands, or on the slopes above mainland cliffs. The shearwaters' main enemy is the Great Black-backed Gull. In order to avoid this predator, the shearwaters stay out to sea in daylight hours, or stay inside their burrows. The chicks are hatched in the borrows and stay underground for ten weeks or so, being fed by both parents. The chick grows very fat. The adults then stop feeding the chick. After about ten days the chick comes out of the burrow one night and crawls downhill. As the nest is normally on a cliff or at the top of an island, downhill usually takes it to the seashore. If it does not, the gulls will eat it. The chick swims out to sea when it reaches the water.

DIVING BIRDS

Many of the birds already mentioned as nesting on moors or cliffs are diving birds. They feed by plunging into the water to catch fishes, sometimes from high in the air. Cormorants, shags, razor-bills, guillemots, gannets, shearwaters, divers, terns, auks, puffins and penguins are some of the diving birds.

Some of these birds dive from high in the air, some dive from just above the surface of the sea and some dive from the surface of the sea itself. Some birds can dive quite deep into the water while others just skim into the surface layers. Gannets can dive quite deep, but gulls can only make very shallow dives. Some birds swoop down and take fishes from the top of the water. Skimmers fly just above the surface, scooping up water and food in their beaks.

A diving gannet is an awe-inspiring sight. The bird is a large one, with a wing-spread of about 180cm. It has a long, razor sharp beak. When it spots a fish from high up in the air, it dives down head first like an arrow. It enters the water with hardly a splash and it stays underwater for at least five seconds. The terns dive out of the sky in the same way as the gannets, but they cannot stay under the water for as long. Diving Petrels and Little Auks both dive into the sea direct from flight. They hold their wings still as they enter the water, then continue to fly under the surface. They use both legs and wings to propel themselves through the water.

Above: The Black Guillemot *Uria grylle* dives into the water from just above the surface. It swims under water with its wings and its feet, and can stay down for as long as one and a quarter minutes. It eats small fishes, and bottom living crustaceans and molluscs.

Left: The Gannets are found all over the world. This is the Australian Gannet, *Sula serrator*. All the gannets are superb divers, able to dive from high in the air.

The birds which dive from just above the surface, or from the surface, use their wings only to move through the water. They simply carry on flying, through water instead of through air. Some of them are adapted to underwater movement. The penguin, which cannot fly and is so clumsy on land, is an elegant, streamlined bird in the sea. It 'flies' gracefully along underwater.

The storm petrels are delightful birds. They are about the size of a house martin and flitter through the air rather like bats. They are named after Saint Peter because some of them seem to walk on the water. When they are feeding, they fly just above the surface of the water with their legs dangling down and pattering on the sea.

Right: The Magellan Diving Petrel, *Plautus magellani* chasing a fish under the water. As the picture shows, this little bird simply flies through the water after its food. The diving petrels are coastal birds, not travelling too far from the shores.

The cormorants are large dark birds which can spend a long time under water. They can stay down for as long as half a minute. When they are not flying or diving they spend a lot of time standing on rocks with their wings half open, drying them. Cormorants are often found fishing in inland lakes.

The cormorant is one of the few birds that are put to work by Man. In the Far East they have been used to catch fish for many centuries. The fishermen put a ring round the bird's neck so that it cannot swallow any fish it catches. They then go out in boats at night, taking several cormorants with them. There is a light in the front of the boat that attracts the fishes. The cormorants dive off the side of the boat with a string attached to their collars. They dive after the fishes, catch some and return to the boat. The fish has been swallowed, but it will not go past the ring on the neck and the fisherman can remove it.

Right: The Common Cormorant, *Phalacrocorus carbo* dives from the surface of the water, or from rocks just above the surface. They fly low across the water, looking for fishes. The cormorants have webbed feet which they use to swim under the surface. The cormorant (*above*) is used to catch fishes in the Far East. It dives into the water wearing a collar and is attached to a boat.

LONG DISTANCE FLIERS

Seabirds seem to be able to stay at sea for ever. Most of them are very good fliers, can glide on wind currents for hours, can dive down and take their food from the sea and can rest on the surface of the sea when they are tired. It is not surprising, therefore, to discover that many of them are great roamers and make nothing of flying round half the world. The extent of their journeys was not known until ornithologists began to put rings on them.

Bird-ringing is a way of telling one bird from another and a way of finding out where they go. The ring is put on the bird's leg. It has a number and an address on it. If the bird is found dead, or caught by another ornithologist, or even shot, the ring is sent to the address on it with details of where it was found. In this way it is possible to find out about the bird's travels, migration routes and so on.

Below: This map shows the journey of the Short-tailed Shearwater, *Puffinus tenuirostris.* These small birds breed in southern Australia and fly round the Pacific Ocean, making use of the prevailing winds.

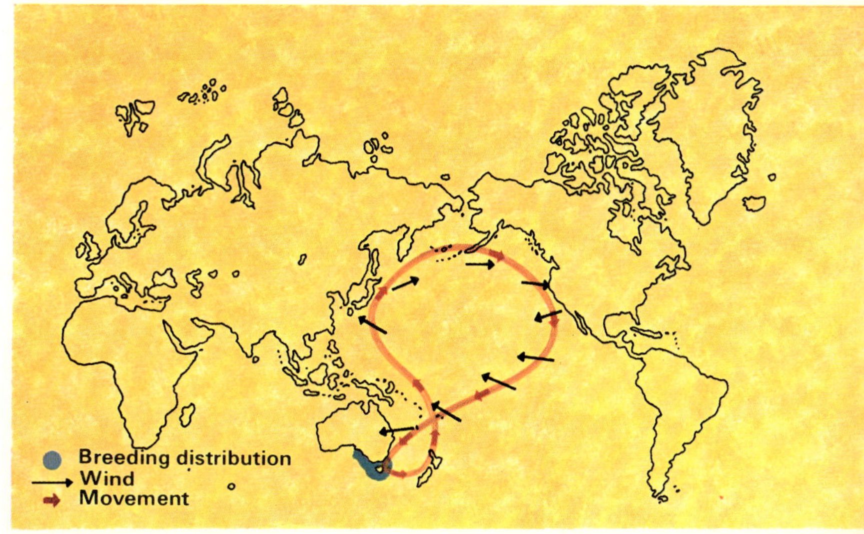

Left: The Short-tailed Shearwater is also known as the Mutton Bird, because its flesh tastes rather like mutton. In Australia and New Zealand the bird is eaten, its stomach oil used in drugs and cosmetics and its feathers used for down.

Birds are able to navigate about the world. They can tell both the time of day and their position from the Sun. Some birds are better at this than others; the pigeon is so good that Man uses it to carry messages. Some of the seabirds are even better than the pigeon.

The albatrosses are real long distance fliers. They are large birds with long, narrow wings, well able to make use of every wind current and eddy. They spend most of their lives gliding over the seas, hardly bothering to flap their wings at all. The Wandering Albatross, which has a wing span of 370cm, ranges over the whole of the Southern Hemisphere. Even while these birds are feeding their chicks, they may make flights of 3,000 kilometres (2,000 miles) or so.

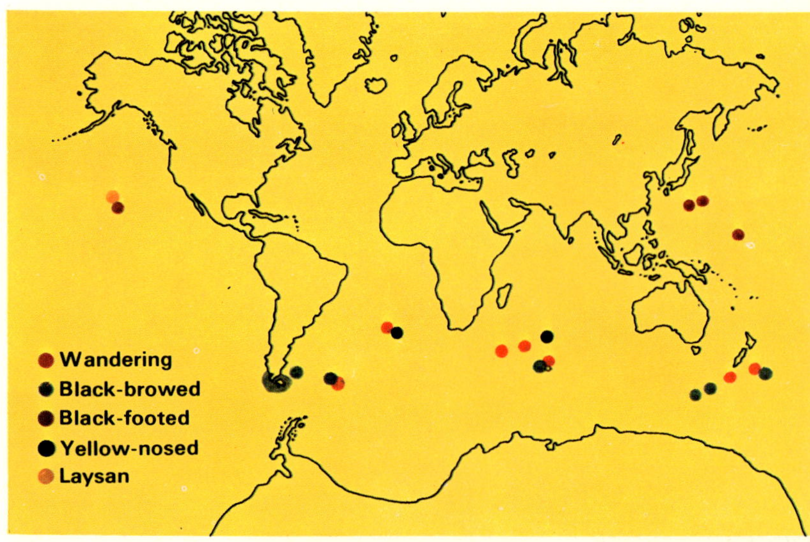

The little shearwaters are impressive travellers too. The Manx Shearwater nests on islands off the coast of Wales and feeds in the Bay of Biscay. Manx Shearwaters have been carried great distances and released to see how long it takes them to get back to their islands. One bird took 14 days to fly from Venice to her island. Another one returned from Boston in North America in record time. The Short-tailed Shearwater is another real long distance flier. The bird breeds in southern Australia. It then flies to New Zealand, across the sea to the Asian coast, along the coast of Alaska, down the west coast of North America and across the Pacific Ocean to its breeding ground. That journey is round the better part of the Pacific Ocean. It is 32,000 kilometres (20,000 miles).

Above: Some of the shearwaters. (*From top to bottom*) Audubon's Shearwater, *Puffinus lherminieri*, Black-vented Shearwater, Sooty Shearwater, *Puffinus griseus* and the Persian Shearwater.

Right: Another North Pacific Albatross, the Black-footed Albatross, *Diomedea nigripes.* This bird will eat almost anything, and is called the feathered pig.

COLLECTING ON THE SEASHORE

All the way through this book it has been emphasized that the most useful way to find out about the seashore communities is to go and look. The animals can be identified with the help of the books called keys. In order to identify the plants and animals, it may be necessary to pick them up, and take them home; to collect them, in fact. The essential equipment for this is several small jars, some plastic bags, a net, perhaps a strong piece of metal to help to move rocks, and very sharp eyes.

However, there are also some strict rules to be upheld. The first is simple. If you do *not* need to study a plant or animal at home, do not take it from the shore at all. Don't take what you don't need. If it is possible to return the specimen alive to the shore when you have identified it, do so. There are many collectors about these days, and if everyone took a specimen away, the beaches would rapidly be emptied.

The second rule is easy as well. Put things back the way they were. If you turn over a stone to see what is underneath, turn it back before you go on. If you do not, the plants and animals on it may die. Try to make as little disturbance as possible.

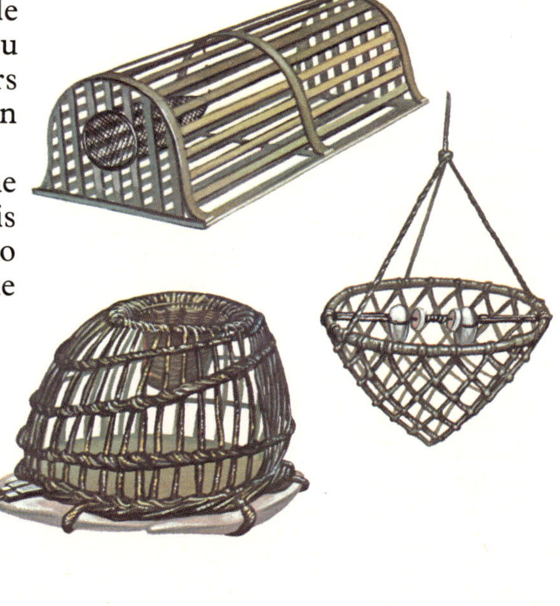

Below: Seashore animals are not always collected because they are of scientific interest. Many of them are very good to eat. The hoop net (*centre*) and the two pots are for catching lobsters. They are put down near rocks.

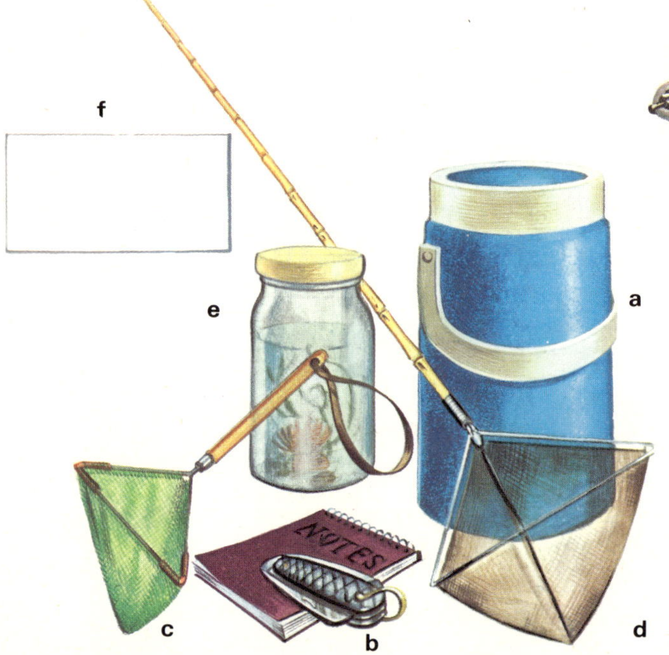

Left: The beach collectors gear. It consists of (*a*) a wide mouth vacuum flask, (*b*) a clasp knife, (*c*) a small hand net, (*d*) a large hand net, (*e*) a wide mouthed plastic bottle and (*f*) a data label. It is important to make a note of where the specimen came from. Most people find that some things are more useful to them than other things. Find out what you use most and take that. Do not carry about anything you do not use.

Left: It is fairly easy to preserve seaweeds. The plants can be brought from the beach in plastic bags. The plants are then arranged on a piece of paper which is under water in a dish. When the plant is spread out, slip it out of the water, making sure it does not move, and cover it with a piece of muslin, or fine cotton cloth. Then put it between blotting paper, white if possible, and dry it slowly under a weight of some sort. When it is dry it may stick to the paper by itself. If it does not, stick down the ends with gummed paper. Write the name of the plant and the place you collected it on a corner of the paper. Store it flat.

If you cannot name the plant or animal on the beach and find you have to take it home, then do not take more than one specimen unless you have a very good reason. If you want to keep an animal alive, do remember that seaside animals cannot live in tap-water. They need fresh seawater. It has to be changed quite often, too. Unless you live by the sea, it will be very difficult. If you want to keep specimens, they have to be preserved. Shells should be cleaned out and dried. Crabs can be kept dried too. Worms, sea-anemones and similar animals can be kept in 5% formalin, in small glass jars.

Right: It is difficult to keep marine animals alive without the proper facilities, such as seawater on tap, but it is possible. The seawater has to be tested frequently to see that it is pH 8·4. That is what the indicator papers are for. Make sure that your live specimens will not eat one another! Many of them can be fed with small pieces of raw meat, as shown here.

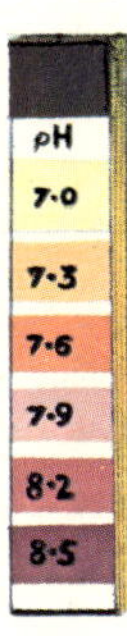

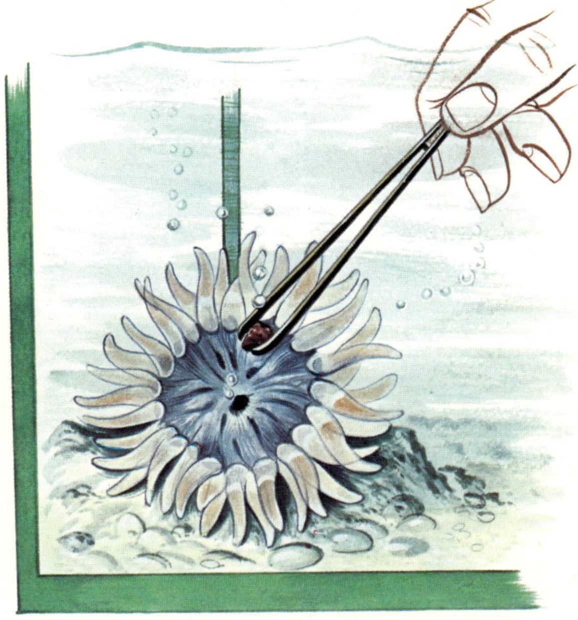

INDEX

*Figures in bold type refer to
illustrations and captions.*

Abalone **35**
Albatross 72, **72**, 73, **73**
Algae 8, 21, 22, 25, 35, **48**
Amphipod **49**
Antarctic 14, 16
Antennae 46
Arctic 57, **57**
Atlantic 15
Auk, 68, **68**
Auklet 63
Avocet 66
Asia 17, **40**

Barnacles 9, 12, **23**, 23, 38,
   53, **53**
Beach Flea **40**
Beetles 22, 40, **40**
Bird-ringing 71
Blennies 35
Britain 15, **34**, 35
Brittlestar 38, 45, 59, **59**
Bullhead **37**
Butterfish **37**

Cameo **34**
Caragheen 24, **36**
Carribean 15, **15**
Central America **41**
Chiton 25, **25**
Clam **17**, 43, **43**, 46, **50**, 51,
   59, 61
Cockle 9, 43, **43**, 46, 49, 51
Cod 56
Comb-jelly 55
Conch **15**, 34, 61
Copepod 21, **37**, 43, 44, 55
Coral **15**, 25, 29, 32, 33, **33**,
   38, 58, **58**
Corallina 37
Cormorant 62, 63, 68, 70, **70**
Cowrie 33, 60, **60**
Crab, **9**, **21**, 31, **33**, 38, **38**,
   46, **46**, 47, **50**, 56, **56**, 75
Cross Cut Carpet Shell **44**
Currents 10, 14, **14**, 15, **15**,
   17
Cushion Star **28**

Dab 56
Diatoms **20**
Dino flagellates **20**
Divers 68
Dogfish 56, **56**
Dolphin 20, 57
Duck 48
Dulse **30**
Dunes 10, **18**, 39
Dunlin 66

Eel 47, **47**, 52, **52**
Eel grass 48, 50
Estuaries **12**, 50–51, **50–51**
Europe 8, 15, **40**

Faroe Sunset Shell **44**
Featherstar 59
Fiord 14

Flatfish 56
Flounder **51**, 52, 56
Foraminifera 11, **11**
Fossils 11
Frilled Venus **60**
Frigate birds **16**
Fulmar 62, 63, **63**, 65
Furbelow **26**

Gannet 63, 65, 68, **68**, **69**
Gaper 46, 49, **50**, 51
Geese 48
Goby **31**, 35, **37**, 47
Greenshank 66
Gribble 53, **53**
Groynes **10**, 39, 46, 53, **53**
Gulf Stream 15
Guillemot 62, **62**, 63, 68, **68**
Gull 8, **40**, 62, 63, 64, 65,
   65, **66**, 67, **67**
Gunnel fish 35

Helmet shell 33, 34
Holdfast 13, 23, 25, 28, **28**,
   32, 39
Humboldt Current 16
Hydra **30**

Iceland 8, **40**
Indian Ocean 14, 17
Indo-Pacific **34**
Invertebrates 8
Ireland 15

Japan 34, **34**
Jellyfish 33, 55, **55**

Kelp 31
Key 9, 27, 35
Kittiwake 62, **65**

Lagoon **50–51**
Lapwing 66
Larvae 21, **21**, 55, **55**
Lichen 22
Limpets **9**, 23, 24, 25, **25**, 27,
   29, 35, 36
Lobster **30**, 33, 38, **38**, **55**
Lobster pots **74**
Lumpsucker 35

Marram grass 39, 40
Mediterranean **34**
Mermaid 57
Mullet 52
Murex shell **59**
Mussel 46, **50**, 51, **53**

Nematodes 28, 43
Nemertines 28, 43
New Zealand **34**
North Atlantic Drift 15

Octopus 35, 56, **56**
Ormer 33, **35**
Otter shell **44**
Oyster 51
Oyster catcher 66

Pacific 14, 52
Pearl 34
Penguin **17**, 68, 69
Perch 52
Periwinkle **9**, **19**, 22, 23, 24,
   25, 27
Petrel 63, 68, 69, **69**
Phalerope **49**, 66
Phosphorescence **20**
Phytoplankton 20, **20**, 21
Piddock 53
Pier 51, 53, **53**
Pipe fish 48
Plaice 56
Plankton **11**, 43, 55, **55**, 58
Plover 66
Pod weed 27
Polyp 32
Portuguese Man-O-War 55, **55**
Prawn 38, **38**, 46, 51, 61
Protozoans 21, **21**, 44
Pollack 52
Porpoise 57
Puffin 63, **63**, 64, 68

Quahog 46, 61

Rayed artemis **44**
Rayed Trough Shell **44**
Razor Shell 43, **44**, 46
Razor-bill 62, 68
Redshank 66
Reef 32, 33, **48**, 58, **58**
Rockling 35

Sanderling 66
Sandhopper 23, 40, 43, 51
Sand-Masons 43, **45**
Sand-piper 66
Sailor-by-the-Wind 55, **55**
Salmon 52
Sargasso Sea **52**
Scallop 46, **47**, 60
Scandinavia 8, **34**, 35
Scots lovage 22
Sea-anemone **21**, 28, 29, 32,
   33, **33**, 38, **38**, **52**, 55, 75
Sea-campion 22
Sea-cow 57
Sea-cucumbers 45, 59
Sea-gooseberry **54**, 55
Sea Hare **49**
Seal 57, **57**
Sea-lavender 22
Sea Lemon **29**
Sea Lettuce 22, **25**, **49**, 50,
   51
Sea-lion 57
Sea Mouse 47, **48**
Sea Oak **27**
Sea Otter 57
Sea Potato **46**
Sea Slater 22, **23**
Sea slug **29**, 32, **32**
Sea-snail 27
Sea spider 33, 38
Sea-squirt 25, **28**, 29, **32**, 61
Sea-swallow 64
Sea urchin **8**, 31, 33, 41, 45,
   46, 53, 59
Seaweed, brown 22, **22**, 23,
   24, **24**, 26, **26**, 27, 31, **31**,
   37, 50, **50**

Seaweed, green 22, **22**, 23,
24, 26, 27, **36**, 37, 48, 50
Seaweed, red 22, 23, 24, **24**,
25, 26, **26**, 27, **30**,
31, **36**, 37
Seaweed Runner **39**, 40
Shag 62, **62**, 68
Shannies 35
Shearwater 64, 65, 67, 68,
71, 73, **73**
Shingle 10, 12, **12**
Shrimp, Brown **21**, **37**, 47,
47, 51
Siphons **42**, 43, 46, 56
Skua 64, **64**, 65, **65**
Snails 48, **58**
Smolt **51**
Sole 56
South Africa **35**
South America 16
Southern Ocean Current **17**
Sponge 25, 29, **29**, 33, 53,
58, **58**, 59
Squid 35
Starfish 31, 33, 38, 41,.45,
46, 59, **59**, 60
Stickleback 52
Striped Sunset shell **41**
Stromb 34
Sunstar **59**
Swan 48

Tellin **9**, **15**, **41**, 46, **49**, 51
Tangleweed 32
Tentacles 28, 32, 35, 38, 45,
46, 61
Tern 64, 65, **67**, 68
Thong weed 27
Thrift 22
Tide, neap 26
Tide, spring 18, 26, 30
Topshells 24, 25, 27, 28, **28**,
29, 33, 34, **34**
Triton Pacific **61**
Trout **51**, 52
Trumpet-shell 34, 51
Turban shell 58
Turtle 56

Venus shell **42**, 43
Vertebrates 8
Volute 61

Wader **49**
Walrus 57, **57**
Wampum **46**, 61
Wedge-shells 43, 46
Weever fish 47, **47**
West Wind Drift 16
Whale-bird 63
Whales 35
Whelk 25, 28, **28**, **31**, 33, 38,
48, 49, **49**
Worm **26**, 28, **28**, 29, **29**, 31,
32, **32**, 38, **38**, 41, 42–43,
42–43, 44, 45, **45**, 46, 47,
48, 49, 53, **53**, 61
Worm-cast **42**
Wrack **18**, **22**, 23, **23**, 24, **24**,
26, 27, **27**, **36**, 50, **50–51**
Wrasse **31**, 35

Xerophytes 22